Outdoor Repairs

BY THOMAS PHILBIN

GROSSET
GOOD LIFE
BOOKS

PUBLISHERS • GROSSET & DUNLAP • NEW YORK

Acknowledgments

Cover photograph by Mort Engel

The author wishes to express his appreciation to the following companies and associations for information or illustrations used in the preparation of this book: American National Standards Institute; Benjamin Moore; Bilco; Buster Crabbe Pools; Celotex; Devcon; Dur-A-Flex; Johns Manville; Louisiana Pacific; National Paint & Coatings Association; Pittsburgh Paint; Portland Cement Association; Sakrete; Sears, Roebuck; Toro; United Gilsonite.

The photographs on pages 25, 26, 27 (top two), 28, 30, 31 (top left), 34, 60, 61, 62, 63, 64, 93, are by Bob Feuchter.

Instructions and safety precautions in this book have been carefully checked for accuracy. However, the author and publisher do not warrant or guarantee results and cannot be responsible for any adverse consequences resulting from the use of information contained herein. The author has attempted to assist the reader in avoiding problems by setting forth appropriate and recommended procedures.

Contents

1
ABC's of Painting the Outside of Your Home

Doing your own exterior house painting can save you a lot of money. Labor is normally 75 percent to 80 percent of the cost of the job, and jobs start at around $500. Also, you don't need great skills to do a good job. If you take your time, and give the job some tender loving care, you can do quite well indeed.

Unlike interior painting, though, many people don't like to do exterior painting. Perhaps you're one. It is more tiring than doing an interior job (those trips up and down a ladder do add up) and if a house has two stories or more, you have to spend some time high on a ladder. If you find the ladder a bugaboo, I suggest that you do the lower, easily reached portions of the house and hire a contractor to do the top. You can still save a good deal of cash.

Paint

There are two basic kinds of paint available for painting the exterior of your home: latex, which thins and cleans up with water; and oil-base, which uses turpentine or mineral spirits as the solvent.

There has been much discussion in recent years about which kind is better. While we were weaned, as it were, on oil-base paint, latex is our choice today. One advantage of latex is that it can be applied when the siding is damp, such as after a light rain. Another is that you can touch up "holidays" (missed spots) without the touch-up showing. But its big plus is using water as the solvent. This makes it much easier to work with than oil-base.

In general, latex paint for siding is available in flat or low-luster finishes, though a few manufacturers have recently come out with a high gloss. Oil-base is available in a gloss finish only. For trimwork you can get latex and oil-base in semi- and high-gloss finishes. Some companies make paints that are good for both siding and trim.

Buy Good Paint

No matter what type of paint you get, make sure it's a good paint. Bargain basement paint gives bargain basement results. It doesn't hide well, fades quickly, is difficult to apply and — the final indictment against it — it doesn't give as much coverage per gallon (sometimes only half as much) as quality paint.

One way to get good paint is to buy brand names, but you have to take care: Even top brands have lines of varying quality, and the lowest on the totem pole can be little better than bargain paint. The criterion we've always used is price. If a gallon of siding paint doesn't cost at least $8, and a gallon of trim $10, better stay away from it, unless it's a legitimate sale.

If your house requires two coats, either because you're changing from a dark to a light color, or the surface is badly weathered, or you're painting it for the first time, use a primer.

Primers: Primers are formulated to penetrate deeply into siding and trim, providing a smooth base for your finishing coat and good "tooth" — the new paint will adhere better. A variety of types are available for painting everything from wood siding to masonry and metal. Our advice is to ask a knowledgeable paint dealer what would be the best for your situation. In general, an oil-base is best for bare wood, latex for masonry; both can be used on metal.

When working with a primer, tint it slightly to the approximate finish color. Covering will be easier.

One caution about finish paint: Don't be misled by claims of manufacturers about their paint being able to cover any color — say, to cite an extreme example, white over black. Sometimes the paint will cover in one coat, but you really have to be a magician (or a professional) with a brush. Most times the paint simply won't cover. Manufacturers know this, but they gamble that their paint (at a much higher price than normally, of course) will cover most colors; meanwhile, they are able to wave dramatic "one coat covers!" ads.

Color

Color is, of course, an important consideration. You can get finish paint in both custom-mixed and a wide variety of standard colors. In recent years, the custom-mixed colors have been priced about the same as stock colors, so you can get exactly what you want at no extra charge. Be aware, though, that the shade of a color on a chip card will not be exactly the same as on your house. Different surfaces absorb the paint to different degrees, and this, among other things, affects final color.

How Much Paint?

There are involved, Einstein-like formulas for calculating how much paint you'll need to cover a house. These have always struck me as a bit of overkill. Rule of thumb is less taxing. The average house will take 10 gallons of siding paint and 3 gallons of trim (assuming one coat — figure ⅔ the total for second coat). If you require more, you can always pick it up. If you require less, the dealer will take it back and refund your money — but clear this with him beforehand. Of course, he won't do this with custom-mixed. Money-saving tip: Tell the dealer you're going to be buying a lot of paint. He normally will discount brand names at from 10 percent to 15 percent on this basis.

While you're in the store, pick up a few inexpensive, large plastic buckets for mixing. The dealer will also give you free painting hats and mixing sticks.

Brushes Best

The kind of tools you use to paint with depends on what you're painting. For siding it's usually best to avoid rollers. Reason: The time it takes to cut in — paint places where the roller can't reach — cancels out the time saved when using the roller on flat areas. Nylon brushes will work fine with both latex and oil-base paints. Figure a 4-inch brush for siding, a 2½-incher for general trim, and a 2-incher for windows.

Avoid Bargain-Basement Brushes: As with paint, you can get stuck by buying bargain basement brushes. Bristles may be too short, tips blunted instead of flagged (split), handles too short. Again, price is a good indicator of quality. Figure about $7 for a 4-incher, half that for your 2½- and 2-inchers. With proper care, these brushes will last for many years.

For shakes, which have vertical striations, or grooves, a cut-down old brush is good. Don't use a good brush — you'll kill it. Or, you can use any of the many pad-type painters on the market. With these, you dip the pad into the paint and wipe it on. They work well.

Roller for Masonry

Rollers do have their place when surfaces are extra rough, such as for masonry, whose textured surface has many minute hills and valleys. A roller with a long nap or fiber works well. Loaded with paint it gets into those hills and valleys. A long-nap of 1½ inches or more is also good for chain-link fence. Sopping wet, those fibers wrap themselves around the links and you can virtually paint both sides of the fence from one side.

For wrought-iron fencing and other detail work, a painter's mitt may work well (we haven't tried it). You wear it like a glove, dipping it in paint and, in effect, paint with your fingers.

Preparation

You've likely heard it before, but it's worth repeating: The key to a good paint job is preparation. The better you prepare surfaces for painting the longer the job will last and the better it will be.

The most common bugaboo is peeling paint. For light peeling, a hook type scraper and wire brush will do nicely. When all unsound paint is off, use a medium sandpaper to feather or smooth the edges of the resulting craters so they don't advertise themselves after you paint.

If your house is peeling or blistering heavily, you might have a moisture problem: Water vapor, migrating through the siding to the outside air, literally pushes the paint off the siding. You can remove the loose paint with high-heat devices of various kinds but we favor an electric sanding tool that you can rent. It has a sanding disc and legs which keep the disc in contact with the wall at the exact depth required without the danger of gouging, something you should be alert to if using a regular portable sander or drill with a sanding attachment. You can rent these devices for very little money at almost any rental outfit. See your Yellow Pages.

Pad type painter is useful for painting shakes, which have vertical grooves, or for painting smooth wood shingles (shown here). Simply dip pad in paint tray and wipe paint on. Pad painters are also available for painting rough materials, such as cement and cinder blocks.

Painter's glove, or mitt, can come in handy for painting a variety of things, such as above. The glove has a plastic liner that prevents paint seeping through to hand.

Long-nap roller is useful for painting rough surfaces.

Hook-type scraper is more useful than regular scraper. For really large peeling areas however, the only solution is a sander.

Ordinary scraper does a good job in taking off light peeling. It is necessary to take all unsound paint off surfaces or new paint will not stick.

All loose paint must be removed. Just as important, if you have a big problem, though, is to diagnose and correct the cause of the symptom. For information on how to do this and correct a variety of other paint maladies, see Chapter 2.

Remove Soil: All heavy accumulations of soil must be removed. A soft bristle brush and a strong cleaning solution followed by a rinse with clear water will do the job. However, you should make sure you're dealing with dirt, not mildew. Mildew is a fungus that doesn't respond to ordinary cleaning. To test, dab pure bleach on the suspect area. If the soil comes off, it means you've got mildew. Ordinary soil will not come off. All mildew must be taken off, or it will grow right through your paint. To do this, mix pure bleach with water and have at it with a sturdy scrub brush. If you have hard-to-reach areas, you can use a push broom. Or, if the problem is really extensive, you can rent an electric brush. After removing mildew, wash down areas with clear water and let dry before painting.

Caulking: Proper preparation also includes caulking the seams of your home. That is, all the areas where there are potential or actual openings: around window frames, between house siding and foundation, at house corners, wherever different materials meet — brick and siding, for example.

There are a number of different caulks available, some of which will last 10 years and more. But these are relatively expensive and only make sense if you intend to thoroughly clean out *all* old, deteriorated caulking, because the new material will only last as long as what's beneath it. A total clean-out is a large job; if you don't want to do it, your best bet is inexpensive oil-base caulk. This will last just as long as the expensive varieties when all old material is not removed.

Leave Some Openings: It is not required — nor desirable — to button up every seam in the house. You should allow some openings to let moisture vapor inside walls escape. Any spots where water can't run in are fine, such as where the bottom of windowsills join the siding.

If siding is damaged, now is the time to minister to it. For a round-up on how to repair

Use sandpaper to smooth edges where peeling paint was removed.

It is necessary, before painting, to caulk gaps where water can enter. You needn't clean out all old caulk unless you intend to use expensive caulk. Not cleaning out and using expensive stuff is a waste — it's only as secure as the caulk beneath it.

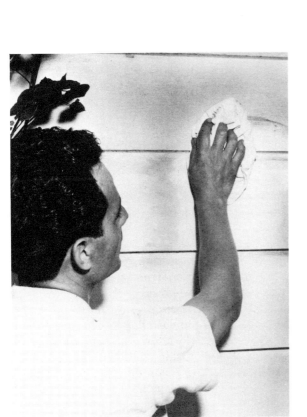

It is not necessary to wash down the entire house, but heavy accumulations of soil should be taken off.

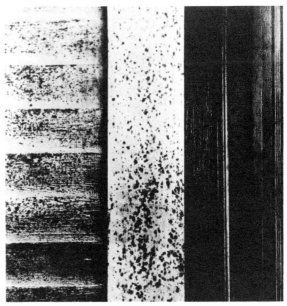

Sometimes mildew is mistaken for dirt. The above is a bad case of mildew. You can test for it by dabbing with pure bleach, which will remove mildew, but not soil.

various kinds, see Chapter 7. If window putty has dried out and cracked, it should also be replaced. Chapter 3 on how to install a window has information on doing this. You should use glazing compound instead of putty, which is passé now. Glazing compound stays flexible indefinitely and normally doesn't crack or dry out as putty does.

Covering Up

Before you start wielding a brush, cover all areas where paint can spatter, such as driveways, walks, shrubbery, and screens. The best covers you can buy are 9- x 12-foot canvas ones. While expensive, they will last a lifetime. Cheaper are various fabric and heavy plastic coverings. Very inexpensive are drop cloths made of super thin plastic. They are very light and susceptible to being blown away, so anchor them at the edges with boards or bricks. The cheapest drop cloth of all is overlapping sheets of newspaper, also weighted down. Screens that are left up may be covered with newspaper secured with masking tape. And do be sure to cover: Paint that gets on concrete or screening is not simple to remove. To save time painting screens, remove them and paint them separately. Just lay them on a couple of sawhorses or boxes.

First step in mixing paint is to stir it a bit with a mixing stick. Concentrate on getting any residue off the bottom.

Pour paint into bucket . . .

Canvas drop cloths are the best coverings you can get, but newspapers or boards will serve just as well.

. . . then back into can. Proceed with this, pouring back and forth, boxing the paint, until it is of uniform consistency.

Painting

Follow label directions for mixing and applying paint. Most have restrictions about at what temperature to paint, how much solvent to use, and the like. Also, try to schedule your work so you don't have to paint in direct sunlight. This is tiresome on the painter and can lead to paint problems you can live without.

Best bet for mixing the paint is to *box* it, as the professionals say: Pour it repeatedly back and forth between two containers until it is the same consistency and color. If you buy it fresh, your mixing job will be easier. Indeed, if you get paint that is lumpy or in which there is a thick residue on the bottom, take it back. Otherwise, you won't be getting the quality you're paying for.

For tinting paint, mix color separately and gradually stir into paint.

Painting Sequence

Paint the second-story trim — windows, eaves, etc. — first, then the siding there followed by the bottom trim, then the siding. In this way, if paint drips, it will not mar finished work. To save time on trim, cut in the entire perimeter framing of all windows with siding paint rather than trim paint. The reverse, cutting in with trim paint, is harder to do.

You can use a standard rung ladder for the job, suspending your paint bucket (and it should have a mouth wide enough to let you get the brush in and out easily) from a hook. Also useful are ladder jacks, which you can rent cheaply. These attach to two halves of a rung ladder. A wide, stout board is laid between them and you have a platform to work from.

In general, when painting, follow these rules.

It is easier, when painting siding and trim, to paint the edge of a window frame with siding paint than with trim paint.

- Use plenty of paint. Not using enough paint is the mistake most beginners make, and skimping leads to missed spots and much more difficult work. Just dip the brush bristles about one third or halfway into the paint, tap it once on each side of the can, and lay it on. Don't mash the bristles. Hold the brush lightly, like something that is alive, letting it and the paint — not your arm — do the work.

Always dip the brush in paint ½ to ⅓ the bristle length, and tap it on inside of can. Avoid wiping brush on can when possible.

Key technique when painting is to go "from the dry into the wet," as the pros say. Start each new stroke 1 foot to 1½ feet beyond wet edge of previously painted area and paint back toward it.

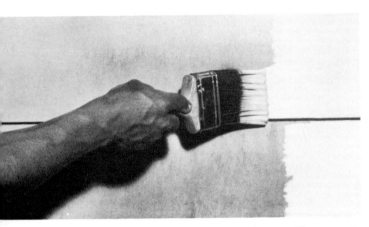

Shown here is the wrong way to apply paint. The new stroke is being started where the previous one ended.

Proper way to paint is first to paint the edge of siding (clapboard is shown), then to paint the face.

- Paint from the dry into the wet. This is the description pros give whereby you start each stroke about a foot and a half from the wet edge of the previously applied paint and paint back toward it. This covers the maximum dry area per each stroke. Once the paint is on, as it were, give it a few light, long strokes, lifting the brush at the end of each stroke to feather or blend areas in rather than leaving blobs.
- Paint small areas at one time. Just paint what you can easily see and reach. It doesn't pay to stretch. This can lead to missed spots and a very fatigued painter very quickly.
- Paint windows from proper angles. When painting narrow parts of windows, just dip the tip of the brush in the paint, stand, and apply at an angle that lets you see the wood well. For example, don't approach the framework that crosshatches the glass head on. If you move to the side a little you'll be able to see more of the wood; this will help you keep your brush on the wood. If you get paint on the glass, wipe it off with a solvent-dampened cloth wrapped around a forefinger.

Painting Siding

If you're right-handed, start painting the siding at the right side of the house, working your way across to the left. Reverse procedure if you are left-handed. From a ladder, the average person can paint a 3-foot-square area from one ladder position. When this area is done, move the ladder and paint an adjacent 3-foot-square area (or whatever you can easily see and reach), overlapping smoothly into the first. Work your way across, painting a horizontal band of the house, then come back and start a new band.

Slightly different brush techniques are required, depending on the kind of siding you have. On clapboard (the smooth boards), first paint the bottom edge of the boards, then paint the face. Remember to use plenty of paint and go from the dry into the wet.

If you are painting smooth shingles, follow the same basic technique as for clapboard. Paint edges of the shingles, then the face, but

You can apply paint to asbestos shingles with horizontal strokes, but you must then make finishing strokes vertical.

make the final, smoothing strokes vertical.

When painting shakes (the vertically grooved material) hit the edge, then apply paint with either cut-down brush or pad painter with vertical strokes.

Most homes have a lot of metal around — decorative fencing, light fixtures, and the like — and it often gets a little rusty or chipped. To paint these items, first use a wire brush or rust remover liquid to remove all traces of rust, then apply a prime coat and a finish paint designed to combat rust.

Cleaning and Storage

If you're just going to be storing brushes or rollers overnight, all you need to do is wrap them in some air-tight clinging plastic wrap.

If you're going to be storing the tools for a long time, they should first be thoroughly cleaned.

To clean a roller, first squeeze out as much paint as possible by running your mixing stick or scraper along the height of the roller all around, letting the paint run into the can. Then, wash the roller thoroughly. If you used latex, do this with warm water and detergent — don't forget the detergent, it's the key to easier cleaning. Then, rinse under warm water, squeeze water out with your hands and store roller wrapped in newspaper.

To clean a roller used with oil-base paint, squeeze paint, then wash in a can filled with solvent used. Do this for five minutes, then discard solvent and rinse roller for another few minutes in fresh solvent.

To clean a brush, place it flat on a sheet of newspaper. Squeeze out excess paint with your scraper or putty knife, working on the bristles from the ferrule, or metal part, to the tips. If latex was used, wash brush in warm sudsy water, wrap, and store.

If you used oil-base paint, you can first squeeze out excess paint as above, then wash thoroughly in thinners you've been using, and store.

A good trick for storing any kind of paint for just overnight is to pour a little of the thinner you're using onto the paint, forming a film that air can't penetrate. No need to put the lid on. If paint is to be stored for long periods, first clean the lip of paint can, then hammer the lid on securely.

To clean oneself, the best thing I've found is a lanolin-based, pink cream. You just wipe it on, let it work for a minute, then wipe it and the paint off with a paper towel. It leaves your skin in better shape than before you painted.

To save energy and avoid mistakes, paint only what you can reach and see easily from one ladder setting.

2
Paint Problems

While paint is a great material for the upkeep of your home, it is not infallible. Problems, little and large, can occur. Some are simple to remedy and some will take hard work to rectify, but it is important in all cases to know why the problems occurred. Only then can you deal with them effectively. Following is a round-up of these problems, why they happen and how to handle them.

Blistering

There are two kinds of blisters — moisture blisters and temperature, or solvent, blisters.

Temperature Blisters: These are less common of the two. They are usually caused by paint being applied in direct sunlight or the temperature being very high. The high heat rapidly creates a dry skin on the paint, and the solvent, which would normally evaporate, has no chance to do so. A clue to having these blisters is that they form quickly after painting — from an hour or two to a couple of days. Usually, the problem occurs more with dark than light paint. To avoid the problem, simply avoid painting in the sun or when it's very hot.

Moisture Blisters: Much more common are moisture blisters. These are caused, simply, by excessive moisture behind the paint. You can diagnose this type of blister by puncturing one: A little water may run out. Of course, if the blisters are long standing, the water may have changed to vapor and escaped.

If moisture is causing the problem, you have to find out where it's coming from. It can come from inside the house. Moisture, in the form of water vapor, is generated by showers, baths, cooking, and so on. If it becomes trapped inside walls it seeks the path of least resistance, permeating the siding and then pushing the paint off the siding on its way out.

To minimize moisture from these sources, you can equip high moisture areas, such as the laundry and bath, with exhaust fans. If at one time a lot of water vapor is being produced, simply opening a window can help. Another solution is to install vents in the siding. One type is a hollow tube that you drive in with a nail; then you pull out the nail. Another is a miniature plastic vent. Red Devil makes them. You drill 1-inch-diameter holes between studs (vertical wall framing members), installing them about 5 inches below ceiling

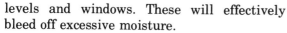

Test panels show bad case of blisters. These may be temperature blisters or moisture type; the latter is far more common.

Peeling. If paint is peeling to the degree shown, the only solution is to remove paint down to the bare wood. You can rent a sanding machine that will let you do the job with minimal difficulty.

levels and windows. These will effectively bleed off excessive moisture.

Sneaky Source: Of course, excessive moisture can occur when water flows directly into walls inside the walls. Missing caulk, insufficient flashing, missing roofing, and the like are suspect here. One sneaky source: Siding that is too close — within 6 inches — to the ground can pull moisture into itself by capillary action.

If open spots are the problem, seal them up as required. For roof and flashing repair, see Chapter 10. If siding is too close, tacking plastic sheeting to the bottom of the siding can help.

Before painting, all blisters, which are just a preliminary stage to peeling, must come off. Tips in the preparation section of the painting chapter tell how to do this.

Alligatoring

This malady gets its name from the way the paint looks — split up into segments like alligator skin.

The most common cause is that incompatible paints were applied. The top layer does not swell and shrink the same way the bottom layer does, so the top layer cracks.

To cure this problem, you usually must take the paint off to bare wood, because the segments eventually develop deeper splits, curl up at the edges, and destroy any paint above it. However, if the problem is slight, you can sometimes avoid a massive removal job by painting with a paint compatible with the top coat. And crossing your fingers.

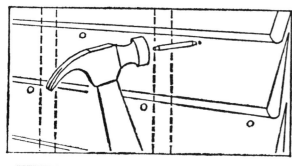

There are a few ways to bleed excessive moisture from inside walls. One tube device (above) is driven into siding with nail which is then withdrawn.

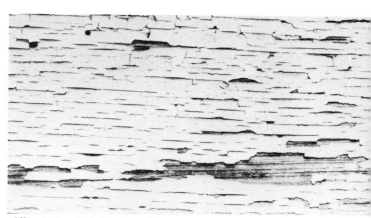

Alligatoring. This is paint alligatoring in an advanced stage. It has split into segments resembling alligator skin, has curled up on the edges and is flaking off the surface.

Chalking. Note how the pigment in the paint has washed down from siding onto brick. Some chalking is natural in paints, but if it shows, it's abnormal.

Chalking

This problem is characterized by staining; it looks as if the paint from an upper area has washed down over a lower one. And indeed it has — the pigment has been leached out of the paint and washed down.

There are three common causes of pigment washdown: (1) Badly weathered wood was not primed properly; the wood absorbs the binders (chemicals that hold the formula together) and the pigment washes away. (2) Cheap paint was used and didn't have enough binders in it. (3) Paint was put on below temperature recommended on label.

The answer is to wash the affected areas, and apply a good primer. Of course, one must make a distinction here between normal and abnormal chalking. Some oil-base paints are formulated to chalk very gradually to keep the job fresh looking. But if the chalking is noticeable, then you've got a problem.

Crawling

This occurs when you apply paint. The paint puddles up, like water on a greasy plate. In-

deed, a heavy accumulation of oily, greasy soil is usually the culprit. Solution: Use a strong detergent to take it all off, then rinse, and let dry.

Spotting

Here, sections of the paint lose either gloss or color. Reason: skimpy application. Solution: none, really. With time the spots will blend in with the rest of the paint as it loses gloss and color. One no-no: Don't apply another coat of paint right away. This can lead to a too-quick accumulation of paint which, in turn, leads to wrinkling.

Cracking

This is the term used for incipient alligatoring. The solution — painting over — was discussed earlier.

Wrinkling

Here, the paint looks like aluminum foil was crushed and then spread flat. Cause: Too-thick application of paint. Solution: Use 60- or 80-grit sandpaper in power sander to smooth spots out.

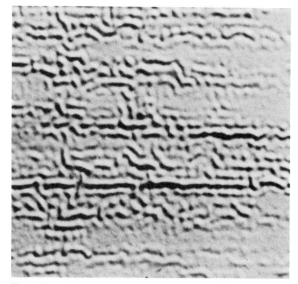

Wrinkling. When paint is applied too thickly, wrinkling can occur. Solution here is to use medium-grit sandpaper to take off excess paint.

3
How to Replace a Broken Window

Replacing a broken window is a relatively easy job for the beginning handyman or woman, and can save the $15 or $20 a glazier would charge. The hardest part of the job is cutting the new glass, and you don't need to do this. Glass shops will do it in seconds to the exact size you specify.

The instructions and photos show a small pane being replaced, but the information is applicable to large panes as well.

Remove Broken Glass Carefully

First step is to remove the broken glass. Wear a pair of work gloves (cotton ones are good), gently rocking the broken pieces in the frame until they lift out. In some instances it will be necessary to break the glass a little more to be able to grip it. Use a hammer, but wear sunglasses or other protection when doing this. To save later clean-up, you can hold a piece of cardboard or a box underneath the window to catch the glass.

Next, use a putty knife, scraper, or old chisel to remove all the old putty from the recesses the glass rests in. You'll also notice small triangular pieces of metal in the frame. These are called glazier's points and are what actually holds the glass in place — it isn't the putty. Remove them with pliers or screwdriver, noting their approximate position.

Measuring for New Glass

With all the old glass out, the frame clean, measure the distance between recesses, both horizontally and vertically. Since wood expands and contracts as the weather changes, it's a good idea to get the new pane a fraction smaller than the opening. So, subtract ⅛ inch from each of the measurements. For example, if the vertical measurement in the frame was 11 inches, your vertical measurement would be 10⅞ inches; if the width was 6½ inches, your measurement would be 6⅜ inches. To be on the safe side, take the measurements a few times.

When removing broken glass, wear gloves. You can catch broken bits with a piece of cardboard or box to save later clean-up.

Prime Frame First

Before installing the glass, use a small brush to apply a coat of exterior paint to the recesses. In this way the dry wood will absorb moisture from the paint rather than the new putty you put in, possibly weakening it.

When the paint is dry, set the glass in the opening, pushing it all the way in place. Then use glazier's points (you can buy a box for a few cents) to secure it, pushing these in with a coin, chisel and hammer, or a screwdriver, near where the original ones were. As you're doing this, make sure the glass is snug in the recesses.

Use Glazing Compound

Today, you putty a window with glazing compound, not putty. The compound has several advantages, not the least of which is that it hardly ever dries out.

Different handymen have different ways of applying it. One that is as good as any is to press the material — it comes ready mixed — on in small globs along each recess. Then, holding the putty knife so it is guided by the glass and one edge of the recess, smooth it out to conform to the shape of the putty on adjacent panes. It's likely that you won't be able to do this with the skill of a glazier, but you will be able to get a presentable shape.

Finally, let the compound dry overnight, then apply a coat of paint. Let this dry, then apply a finish coat.

Glazier's points are used to hold glass in place. These should be pulled out and recesses cleaned of all old putty.

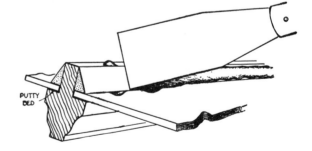

Putty knife should be drawn along to smooth compound as shown. The glass and recess edge steady the knife so you can cut a nice, even bead.

After priming, window is slipped into place. Glass should be cut at glass shop to fit — it's too difficult for a beginning handyman to do.

Apply glazing compound in dabs or form it into thin rolls and press into place.

Glazier's points can be tapped into place with chisel and hammer, or pushed in with any large coin.

Let compound dry overnight, then give it two coats of exterior paint.

How to Replace a Broken Window **19**

4
Gutter Care and Repair

Keeping gutters shipshape is more important than most people realize. Ones that aren't functioning properly can lead to other problems that one can easily live without.

Clogged Gutters

Probably the most common problem with gutters is simply that they get clogged with waste material — twigs, leaves, seeds, and what-have-you. Left alone, this material can build up to the point where the water can't run freely down the gutter. In warm weather, it overflows onto the ground, saturating it; after a while the water can seep through the foundation wall, or perhaps find its way in by cracks. Indeed, excess ground water is a common cause of a damp basement. Also, in warm weather trapped water can become stagnant — a nice breeding ground for mosquitoes.

In winter, trapped water turns to ice, the water can also overflow, but it can also back up under roof shingles and get into the house. This can wreak havoc on walls and ceilings. Or, if water turns to ice, the weight can rip the gutters right off the house.

Clean Out

Gutters should be periodically checked for debris, especially in the fall and spring when waste can accumulate quickly. You can use a small trowel to scoop most of the waste out, then flush the gutter with a hose. As a final treatment, direct a jet stream of water by holding your finger halfway over the hose nozzle down the downspouts to make sure they're cleared.

Incorrect Pitch

Gutters should be pitched, or slanted, so they slope a minimum of 1 inch for every 30 feet of length, or a maximum of 1 inch every 10 feet. If incorrectly pitched, water can also overflow or be trapped in the gutter.

It is very difficult to tell if pitch is correct by eye alone. To check, climb up on a ladder after a rainfall and see if water is standing in the gutter. If so, it's incorrectly pitched. Or, you can simply pour a bucket of water in and see how well it flows to the downspout.

To correct pitch, the first thing to do is establish a perfectly level line on the fascia — the trim board along the top of the house that the gutter is mounted against. This line can then serve as a reference guide to correct pitch. Most handymen who pitch gutters incorrectly do so because they assume the house is perfectly level. Houses settle, though, and are hardly ever level. In essence, you establish your level line as if the house weren't there.

Establishing Level

First, make a mark about an inch below the gutter at the high end, and an inch below it at the downspout end. Drive a nail into the ends of the fascia at these points and draw a line tightly between them. With a helper, and using a level, raise or lower the line until it is perfectly level. When doing this, it is best to hold the level parallel to but not actually touching the line. Touching it can throw it out of level. When level, mark the fascia at the ends where the line is.

Establishing Pitch

Next, check to see if the top of the gutter at the high end is touching the shingles. It should be. If so, simply raise your line and refasten so it is parallel with the bottom of the gutter. Then move the line down at the other end so it runs at the proper pitch, and fasten in place. For example, if the bottom of the gutter on the high end is ½ inch above the level mark, and the gutter is 30 feet long, the downspout end should be ½ inch lower than the other mark — that would give you a 1-inch pitch in 30 feet. If the high end of the gutter happened to be 1-inch above the level mark, the other end guideline could be right at the level mark.

Resetting the Gutter

Next, you remove the gutter and reset. For the job you'll need a number of aluminum

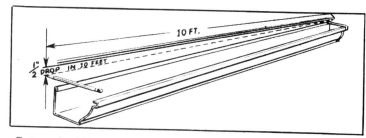

Gutters should be pitched no less than 1 inch for every 30 feet of gutter length, nor more than 1 inch for every 10 feet. Here it would be pitched ½ inch for every 10 feet.

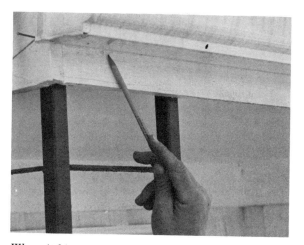

When pitching gutter, high end should touch shingles. Pitch line should be attached to string nailed to fascia and drawn parallel to bottom of gutter . . .

. . . then drawn to downspout end and fastened at position that establishes pitch. Here, correct pitch meant fastening the line lower than fascia.

To unfasten gutter for refastening, use crowbar to tap head of spike out. Then slip claw on bar over spike near head and tap on bar to knock spike out.

Spikes go through ferrules into rafter ends. One spike every other rafter is sufficient.

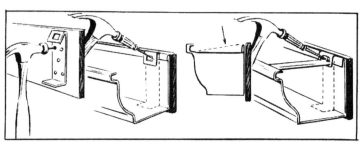

Some gutters are attached with hangers rather than spikes and ferrules. If you replace these, procedure is as follows. 1) Nail brackets to fascia. 2) Slip gutter into bracket, then depress top flange with screwdriver and hammer. 3) Insert strap hanger under front lip of gutter and place strap into bracket hook, then 4) depress bracket hook locking gutter securely in place.

spikes and ferrules (tubes). These lightweight aluminum items are available in lumberyards and building supply stores.

Start at the high end. Using a crowbar and hammer, tap the inside of the gutter to knock out the head of the first spike a little. Then slip the fork of the bar over the spike near the head and rap the bar to drive the spike out all the way. Following this procedure, remove as many spikes — say three or four — as necessary so you can move the gutter enough to realign its bottom with your line.

Fastening the Gutter

To fasten a gutter properly, you drive spikes through the gutter into the ends of the rafters. Some installers secure gutter only to the fascia, but this isn't very secure.

To locate rafter ends, lift up the shingles; the ends will be visible. To drive each spike, first position a ferrule inside the gutter so it falls over a rafter end. Make a starting hole in the outside of the gutter with an awl. Drive the spike through the hole. When you're sure the point is inside the ferrule, drive the spike all the way through into the rafter end. As you do, make sure that the gutter stays at proper pitch. Continue like this down the length of gutter, first loosening, then resetting it.

If, before you started the whole procedure you found that the high end of the gutter was not touching shingles, you should reset it at that point before establishing your level line.

To get the proper pitch on some gutters, the downspout end of the gutter may actually go below the bottom edge of the fascia. In this situation, you'll have to nail a board to the end of the fascia to fasten the guideline to. (This is shown in one of the photos.)

Leaks

A common malady of gutters is that they leak, usually where sections overlap. Reason: They're not overlapped in the right direction. Many times the open joint faces running water. This is like having roof shingles with the open joints facing the roof peak.

If this is the case, it's best to take the gutter down for the job. When reconnecting, use

½-inch No. 6 or No. 7 sheet-metal screws: One on each side and the bottom should do it; but use more if it looks like the gutter needs it. Before fastening, apply a good coat of sealer between sections. Hardware stores sell an aluminum type that is good. Be sure to remove excess sealer that squeezes out. A build-up of this can trap debris and cause water flow blockage.

Downspout Leaks

Leaks at the downspout are usually caused by improper installation of the outlet piece — the lipped fitting on top that connects downspout to gutter proper. Instead of locating it so the lip is on the outside of the gutter, it is installed so it is inside, which seems more logical.

Cure here is to remove the piece (or buy a new one) and reinstall it properly with sheet-metal screws and a healthy bead of sealer.

The end pieces of the gutter can also leak, and these should be secured with screws and sealer.

To minimize the chance of a downspout developing leaks at the joints, make sure it is securely anchored to the house. This prevents movement. Strapping iron and lag screws should be used for anchoring.

The lowest end of the downspout should be a few inches above ground level unless it enters an underground drain. A splash block (a formed piece of concrete) under the end will prevent damage to sod and surrounding shrubbery.

Gutters also develop holes. There are various repair kits for patching these and full instructions are provided. We've used the fiberglass type and it works well.

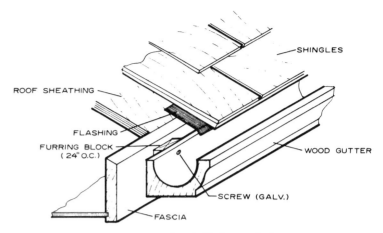

If you have wood gutters, they will probably be attached as above. To unfasten them, unscrew from the blocks mounted on fascia. Blocks are usually 24 inches apart.

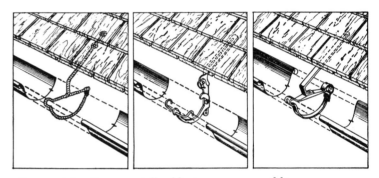

Some metal gutters, especially older types, are secured by means of strips nailed under roofing material. If you can lift the roofing to pry out nails, fine. If not, use a flat pry-bar with a claw — set claw against nail and pound on bar with hammer to sever nail, then cover nail parts with roofing cement. Or you can simply cut off the exposed part of the hanger with a tinsnips.

Prime leakage point is where gutter sections overlap. They have to be lapped so that the open joint faces away from running water.

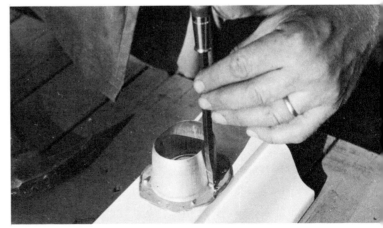

Downspout fitting is fastened to gutter so that fitting lip goes on the outside. Fasten fitting with sheetmetal screws. Use sealer first.

5
Mending Masonry and Asphalt

Concrete, brick, and other masonry materials, while very strong, are not impervious to damage. Weather, the ground heaving (swelling) from frost, improper installation procedures and other reasons can cause it to develop various maladies, mainly cracks and holes. But the solutions, usually, are simple.

Narrow Cracks

Driveways, steps, walks, walls, and other things made of concrete commonly develop hairline cracks. While usually not serious in themselves unless they're in supporting walls, they should be repaired promptly because, left alone, they will get bigger and may necessitate a large job where an entire segment of material — say a section of sidewalk — needs replacement.

For the job you can use a premixed sand mix, such as Sakrete makes, or a masonry paste patcher that comes in a cartridge, such as made by United Gilsonite or Red Devil. The premix is a powder that you mix with water; the paste comes ready for use. Unless you have lots of cracks, the paste will be more convenient.

Preparing the Crack

Before using anything, first clean out the crack thoroughly. Repair material won't stick to a crack that is filled with soil and debris; it has to bond to concrete.

For the job you can use a stiff bristle brush, or wire brush, or you can dig debris out with an old screwdriver, putty knife, or scraper.

To use the cartridge, first clip off the plastic nozzle at a 45° angle with a sharp knife. The wider the bead you want, the closer to the cartridge itself you should cut. Then break the cartridge seal by sticking a long nail down into the nozzle until it penetrates.

Rest the nozzle tip on the crack and squeeze the gun; the repair material will flow out in a neat bead. Move the tip along, pressing down to get the material as deeply into the crack as you can, and also remove air bubbles.

Narrow cracks may be filled conveniently with paste patcher. First clean crack thoroughly with brush and scraper.

Cartridge slips easily into standard caulking gun. Squeezing trigger emits neat bead of patcher.

Patcher is easy to use. Cut spout off at 45-degree angle. The closer you cut to the cartridge, the wider the bead of patcher will be.

As you apply patcher, press on gun so that tip forces patcher well into crack. You don't want to leave any air space.

Smooth patcher with scraper or putty knife. Dip tool into water frequently for easier smoothing.

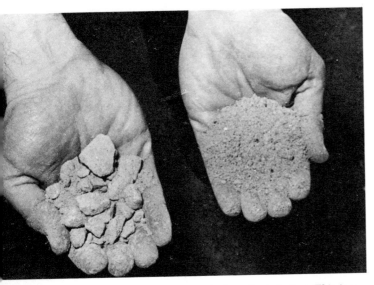

For large cracks, a premixed sand mix is best. This is a smooth sand–cement mixture shown in hand at right. At left is concrete mix, which contains aggregate — rocks. Concrete mix is used principally for building things where cement thickness of over 2 inches is required.

All loose, unsound concrete must be removed. You can tap it loose with a cold chisel (a chisel made of especially hard steel) and a hammer.

First, use a brush, scraper, and your fingers to remove all loose, crumbling material and soil. Examine the edges of the crack. Are they sound? If not, use a cold chisel and hammer to remove hanging parts. You want a solid, clean base to apply the premix to.

Following directions on the bag, mix a batch

Clean out crack. A scraper is useful — and so are your fingers.

When the crack is filled, use a putty knife or scraper to smooth the material. As you smooth, frequently dip the blade into a dish of water. This will make the material spread easier. Then, simply let dry.

Larger Cracks

If you have a large crack to repair, one of the premixed cements is best.

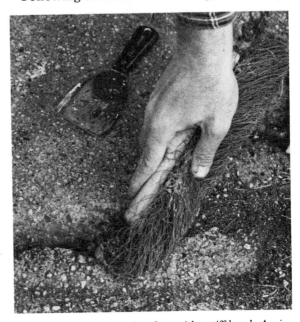

Final preparation of crack is done with a stiff brush. A wire brush works well.

Follow instructions on bag for mixing premix with water. You can pour dry ingredients on spread-out plastic trash bag, make hole in center of premix, then add water.

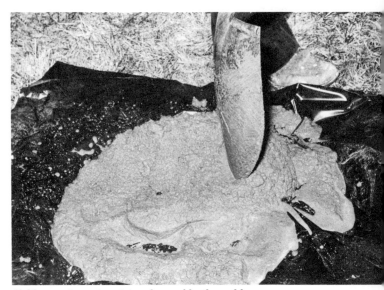

Fold water into mix, mixing thoroughly, then add more water as specified. Amount shown is from a 20-pound bag.

Even handier is a wheelbarrow. It is especially helpful when you have a large amount of mix to prepare.

of the sand mix. Premix comes in various sizes — 20, 45, and 80 pounds, for example — and is not expensive. A 20-pound bag costs less then $2.

Mixing

Best way to mix a large batch is to dump the dry ingredients on a piece of plywood, or a piece of plastic — a large trash bag will do nicely. Stir them thoroughly with a shovel. Then, form the mix into a pile with a hole in the middle. Pour water in the hole and fold in the mix with the shovel. Mix thoroughly, adding water as needed, but don't exceed the amount specified on the bag unless the mix is too stiff. It's too easy to have, at one moment, a mix that is too stiff, and the next, a mix that is soupy. Go slowly as it will pay in the long run.

Wet Crack

Before using the mix, douse the crack with water. The dry concrete will then suck this moisture in rather than the water in the sand mix, weakening it. Then, pack the mix into the crack with a trowel, poking at it to remove all air pockets. Level it with a square trowel or board and then come back an hour or so later

Wet down crack thoroughly, ladle mix into it, filling it completely.

Use trowel to smooth patch. Keep front edge of trowel raised as you pass across patch with semi-circular motions.

and give it a final smoothing with your square trowel. You can buy an inexpensive trowel at hardware stores. Smooth with sweeping strokes, keeping the front, or leading edge, of the trowel raised as you do.

That same day, and for a couple of days thereafter, spray the patch with a fine spray from a hose, or cover it with burlap or cloth and keep that wet. This lets the concrete cure, or dry gradually, and prevents cracking.

When crack is filled, poke at it with scraper or trowel to make sure all air pockets are removed.

Patch is almost finished. After troweling, let stand for an hour, then give it final finish troweling. Wet down patch for a few days so it can cure properly.

To tuckpoint brick, first chip out loose mortar.

Brush spots clean, and wet thoroughly with water.

Push mortar mix into joints. Using trowel as shown makes mortar easier to handle.

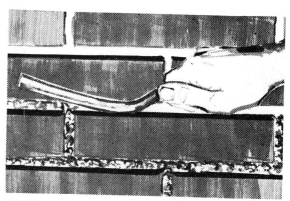

Finally, finish joints to match other joints with jointer, a curved metal tool made for this purpose.

Tuck Pointing Brick

The most common problem with brick is that the mortar that holds it together falls out in spots. The solution is to replace with fresh mortar, a process known as tuck pointing. For the job, you can use one of the premixed mortars or paste patchers. The latter come in cartridges and are available in various colors to match mortar colors.

First, clean out any loose or cracked mortar with a cold chisel. Get all the smaller pieces out by flushing the area with a hose, or use a stiff bristle brush and water.

Prepare the mortar mix, then wet the joints again and press the mortar into the crack with a jointer, an inexpensive curved metal tool. When filled, use the jointer to finish the mortar to match joints on the rest of the wall. After 5 minutes, clean the faces of bricks of excess mortar with a brush, then final-finish with the jointer.

Prepared paste patchers can also be used for tuckpointing. They come in various colors to match mortar color.

Holes or Cracks in Blacktop

Asphalt or blacktop driveways can also develop cracks and holes.

For narrow cracks no more than ¼-inch wide we favor a driveway crack filler in cartridge form. You use it like a paste for concrete. If the crack is more than ½-inch deep, it should first be filled with oakum to within ¼ inch of the surface; oakum is a ropelike material available at hardware stores.

For holes in a driveway, a cold mix patching compound is the material to use. It comes ready to use from the bag.

First, clean out all loose material in the hole, then slightly overfill it by about ½ inch, simply shoveling the patcher in. Then compact the material by pounding on it with the end of a stout board until it becomes level with the surrounding surface.

Resealing Driveway

If your blacktop driveway is somewhat run-down, it may be in line for resealing. Blacktop sealers are commonly available. Application instructions will be on the container. All you do basically is sweep the driveway clean, patch as needed, and apply a couple of coats of the sealer with a roller.

For narrow cracks, asphalt paste patcher is good. First, clean out crack.

Clip end of cartridge and squeeze ready-to-use patcher in crack.

Pack patcher in crack with putty knife or scraper, dabbing tool in water as you do.

Finally, finish patch to blend it with surrounding surface.

If hole in asphalt or blacktop is large, a ready-to-use cold-mix patcher is the answer. Pack it in hole ½ inch higher than surrounding surface, then tamp level with the end of a board.

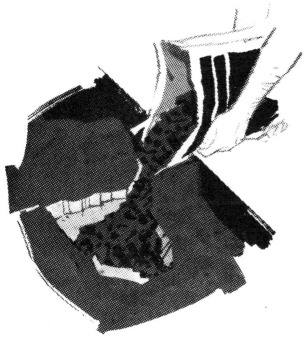

If hole is large, it is possible to pour mix right from bag. If extra large, use a large stone as a filler to conserve material.

Resealing driveway is easy. Using a roller on an extension handle eases it even more.

6
Replacing Bad Concrete

Concrete deserves its reputation as a super-strong, durable material. But who has never seen a concrete driveway, or concrete steps or some concrete structure that has cracked — sometimes badly so?

The reasons for this are usually one or two things: skimpy use of materials and/or improper installation. The potential for strength was there, but it was not realized.

In doing your outdoor repairs, you may find that you have such a situation. If you do, it is important to understand that patches simply won't stick in material that has been improperly installed. The only solution is to tear out the old concrete and replace it with new.

Generally, from the point of view of skills required, working with concrete is not difficult, though you better be prepared to use copious amounts of elbow grease. Only one aspect will throw some handymen: finishing, or smoothing, the concrete. Some people can learn to do this fairly quickly — and some won't. It would pay to practice on a small, out-of-the-way job first. Or, if the whole idea of finishing seems to be beyond you, hire a brickmason for finishing. He'll do a good job in a few hours — and you'll still be responsible for 95 percent of the work.

The best time to do concrete work is in the spring before the weather becomes very hot. Not only will you perspire less, but there will be less chance of premature drying of the concrete by the hot sun. If necessary, the work can be done at any time of the year. Chemical additives make it possible to pour concrete even in midwinter, although this is not recommended for the do-it-yourselfer.

How to Make Concrete

There are two basic ways to get concrete for a job. You can buy it ready-mixed from a truck, or you can make your own. For a large job, ready-mix is the answer. It's relatively cheap, and very convenient. The truck just backs up and pours the material exactly where you need it.

For smaller jobs, ready-mix can be expensive. And if the amount is very small, you can't get a truck to deliver it. For these smaller jobs, the answer is to make your own concrete from scratch. And to do that, quality must be your byword. Inferior quality concrete is high on the list of reasons for concrete failure.

Making the Concrete

Concrete is composed of portland cement (not a brand, but a type of cement), water and aggregates — sand, crushed stone, or gravel. It can be bought with microscopic air bubbles suspended in it, in which case it's called "air-entrained," or without this feature. In areas subjected to freeze–thaw cycles, air-entrained material is a good idea. When pressure is exerted on the concrete the bubbles, rather than the concrete, break and act like safety valves. You make the concrete "air-entrained" by adding special chemicals to the mix.

When buying the components, there are a couple of things to be aware of. First, the cement should be free of lumps. Aggregates, if the coarse kind (sand is characterized as fine) should be sound and hard, not soft and flaky and should be mostly roundish rather than sliver-like. Coarse aggregate size should range from ¼ inch to 1½ inches. The slab being poured dictates the size aggregate allowed — the thicker, the bigger the aggregate. So, driveways, sidewalks and patios can use aggregate up to 1 inch; for slabs that are 5 inches to 6 inches thick, aggregate that is up to 1½ inches is recommended. Good aggregates will strengthen the work. Without it concrete would shrink and crack readily — and the concrete would be much more expensive in the long run.

What Makes Quality Concrete?

The combination of the cement and water is the key to quality concrete — if the concrete is allowed to cure properly. If too much water is used, the "paste" (what the trade calls cement-water combination) will be diluted; but the less water (the less dilution), the stronger the concrete.

The table below gives the proportions of mix to use to make one cubic foot of concrete. The proportions are given in weight, because this is more precise than by volume (half a bucket of aggregate, quarter bucket of cement, etc.).

Making Air-entrained Concrete

Maximum Size of Aggregate	Cement (lbs.)	Sand (lbs.)	Coarse Aggregate (lbs.)	Water (lbs.)	Makes
⅜ in.	29	53	46	10	1 cu. ft.
½ in.	27	46	55	10	1 cu. ft.
¾ in.	26	42	65	10	1 cu. ft.
1 in.	24	39	70	9	1 cu. ft.
1½ in.	23	38	75	9	1 cu. ft.

To find out what to use, check the size of the aggregate. When you've found the largest pieces, you know how much aggregate, cement and water to use by reading across the table.

One cubic foot of concrete is small enough to mix by hand. But for machine mixing, the only way to go for any fair sized project (steps, sidewalk) is machine mixing. Indeed, you can't use air-entrained concrete if you don't use a machine. To get proportions for your mixer, just multiply its capacity — say, 3 cubic feet — by the amounts needed for one cubic foot.

There is a formula for determining how much concrete you need, but telling your dealer the dimensions of your project is just as easy. You can always return anything you don't use. One other tip: You can use a bathroom scale to weigh out ingredients.

Mixing

To machine-mix concrete, first pour all the aggregate (up to the capacity designated) and half the water into the mixer. If an air-entraining agent is used, add it now. Start the machine, then add sand, cement, and remaining water.

When thoroughly mixed, test the concrete. If it is okay, it should be just wet enough to stick together without crumbling and should slide down rather than run off the shovel. If the mix is too wet (soupy), add aggregate and sand until it is okay. If too stiff, reduce the amount of sand and aggregates in the next batch. If too sandy or stony, decrease these ingredients next time. One cardinal rule of concrete mixing is never to add only water to a mixture that is too stiff. That can quickly ruin it.

In the event you're not going to use air-entrained concrete, use different proportions when mixing, as follows:

Making Regular Concrete

Maximum Size Coarse Aggregate	Cement (lbs.)	Sand (lbs.)	Coarse Aggregate (lbs.)	Water (lbs.)	Makes
⅜ in.	29	59	46	11	1 cu. ft.
½ in.	27	53	55	11	1 cu. ft.
¾ in.	25	47	65	10	1 cu. ft.
1 in.	24	45	70	10	1 cu. ft.
1½ in.	23	43	75	9	1 cu. ft.

New Driveway

First step in installing the driveway is to break up and remove all the old concrete down to the bare earth. This is not easy work, but there are a couple of tricks to minimize the muscle output.

The job is done with a sledgehammer. Pick one that's not too heavy for you. They come in various sizes, starting at around 6 pounds and going up in two-pound increments. Heft them in the store and find out which one you handle most easily.

In action, raise the hammer and let it fall of its own weight on the concrete; don't drive it. Aim for the edges of the pieces of concrete, breaking off small, manageable pieces rather than trying to break a piece from the middle.

If you encounter tree roots while chopping, cut completely through them with a saw and discard them. Roots are sometimes the culprits in cracking a concrete driveway.

A driveway that has seen better days. Problem was that concrete was only 2 inches thick and was cracked by pressure of earth swelling from frost.

Before you start breaking up the concrete, you should arrange for getting rid of the broken pieces. If you have an old cesspool that's no longer in use, it will provide the ideal space. You can just haul the pieces to it (by wheelbarrow) and toss them down. If you are going to haul it away yourself, it's a good idea to pull the truck as close to the driveway as possible. If you have no way of removing the material yourself, generally you can hire someone to carry it away for you.

There are various ways to build a driveway, but many of them involve really haphazard craftsmanship and result in cracked concrete. The one described here will take a little longer to build, but it won't be cracked five or six years from now. It consists of a two-inch base of sand and four inches of concrete reinforced with wire mesh. The concrete "floats" on the sand so that in time of heavy frost when the ground swells and applies pressure, the slab will yield with it and crack.

The driveway should run as straight as pos-

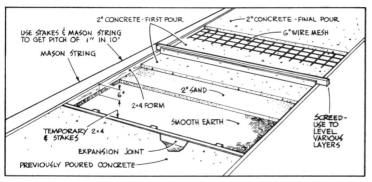

Details on building a driveway that will last.

sible from the garage to the street and pitch slightly downhill for drainage. If your land is naturally sloped, this will not be a problem. If the land is almost level, you can either pitch the driveway downhill or crown it up — that is, make the concrete rounded and higher in the middle than at the sides so water runs off to the lawn on each side. (More about this later.)

Install Forms

Next, install 2 x 4 form boards. These should be as straight as you can buy (sight down them from one end to the other to determine that they have no twists or warps).

Assuming you're using the dimensions of an existing driveway, use a square-edged spade to dig out the sod on either side of the driveway to the depth (plus ½ inch) and width of the 2 x 4s, forming ledges. Save the soil. Then insert the boards end-to-end in the recesses.

Next, fasten a mason's string on both sides of the driveway, to the top of the form boards at one end, and to stakes driven into the ground at the sidewalk end. Level the string with a line level. The strings will serve as guides to the outer edges of what will be the concrete slab. Then align boards with strings as your guide for making straight edges.

Next, install the forms permanently. They should have their inside edges aligned with the strings, and be pitched at a minimum rate of 1 inch for every 10 feet. By measuring between the string and the tops of forms you can tell if they're descending at proper pitch. Use your foot to hold each board in the proper position, bending it up or down slightly if necessary, and secure it by nailing it to 18-inch stakes driven into the ground. Use a stake every 3 or 4 feet and wherever form boards butt (come together).

Once the boards are staked in place, pack soil behind them so the poured cement will not exert pressure and throw them out of position.

Excavating

Remove the soil to a depth of 6 inches (from the tops of the form boards) over the entire driveway. Use a large rake to smooth the ground.

After this, add the sand base. To find out how

A screed in action. It is basically a straight board with another board nailed on so you can level sand and concrete

A screed can be simply a board, such as the one used on small job here.

much you need, give the dimensions to a building supply dealer — so many square feet at a 2-inch depth — and have it delivered to the site by truck.

When the sand is dumped on the driveway, spread it out, then build a screed (detailed in sketch) to level it to the required depth. To use the screed, grip it in the middle and push it back and forth as if you were taking excess frosting off a cake.

Wire Mesh

The wire mesh placement is calculated next. Obtain a sufficient quantity of ⅛-inch wire (6-inch squares). Cut it (with snips) to fit over the driveway in a neat patchwork, then lay the pieces to one side in the arrangement you put them in.

After this you should decide where to put the expansion joint strips. These are strips of asphalt-impregnated material that are installed across the driveway to segment it into sections. (One very long monolithic mass of concrete is more susceptible to cracking.)

You should not have more than 30 feet of unsegmented concrete. Since you will pour next to the garage slab, it should be part of your calculations. For example, if the garage slab were 20 feet long, you would only be allowed to go another 10 feet before making a joint. Also, use one strip at the edge of the garage-floor apron.

Once the placement is decided, install each strip (for most driveways one plus the apron strip will suffice) backed up by a staked-in-place 2 x 4. The 2 x 4s will prevent the concrete from knocking the strips over.

Pouring the Concrete

There are a couple of ways to pour the concrete. First, lay bricks and blocks flat on the sand. Lay the mesh on, in proper position, then pour the concrete. Wear rubber boots and work with a shovel to spread it out to eliminate air bubbles. Then use a screed (this time constructed to level at 2 inches) to level it even with the tops of your forms.

The other way is to pour the first two inches, lay the mesh on and let the concrete set, then make the final 2-inch pour and level off. Either of these ways will serve you well. Remove any braces for the expansion-joint material immediately after the final pour.

Easiest way to pour concrete is to have someone else do it — get it delivered ready-mixed in truck. If you wish, you can hire mason for finishing portion of job.

Finishing the Concrete

There are two types of finishes, or textures, commonly given a concrete driveway: smooth and rough. The smooth finish is done with a steel trowel; the rough finish is done with a wood float, which looks like a big wooden trowel.

When using either, you have to do the job when the concrete is just at the right stage; when it's neither still soupy nor too dry. If it's too wet, your tool will gouge furrows in it; too hard, and you'll have to exert too much pressure.

To avoid this, start troweling when all the water has disappeared from the surface. If using a steel trowel, make semicircular half-moon sweeps with the front or leading edge of the trowel raised. If using a float, use the same motion; you needn't raise the leading edge.

When the body of the driveway is finished, go over the edges. There are special small edging tools that you run along the edge to round it off.

For smooth surface on concrete, steel trowel is used. For rough surface, a wood float is used.

Let Concrete Cure

In order to give concrete its maximum strength, you need to let it cure, or dry, gradually. Let it harden overnight. The next day (you can remove form boards with a pick), give it a fine spray from a hose, and keep it wet for three or four days by spraying occasionally.

Finally, fill the gaps left by the form boards with soil, and sprinkle on some grass seed.

Crowning Up

If the grade of your property is such that pitching it properly is impossible, you can crown it up. Cut a screed to a gradual contour with a maximum depth of one inch in the middle. Pour the concrete and run the screed over it in the normal way. It will leave the concrete higher in the middle than at the sides, and water will run off easily to the sides.

If your driveway is curved, your form work will be different. Use 1 x 4 lumber. Form short radius curves with hardboard or ¼-inch plywood. Stake forms more closely at curves.

Concrete Steps

If you need to replace concrete steps, the first procedure, as with a driveway, is to break up the old ones, including any footing. Save the broken concrete. It will be useful as fill.

Footings

The new steps will require footings so they won't sink. There are various ways of doing this, but one concrete-saving trick is to dig two or more 6- to 8-inch diameter postholes below the bottom tread and fill them with concrete. Holes should extend at least 6 inches below the frost line. (Your local building code authorities can tell you what this is.) Also, tie the top step or landing to the foundation wall with two or more metal anchors.

Forms

Forms for steps may be built with plywood or boards. When building them, brace rigidly to prevent bulging or concrete leaking. The boards should be straight and free from imperfections that would be visible in the hardened concrete. Build the side sections of the forms first, staking them in place. Then, nail on riser sections, starting at the top.

As you go, check with a level to allow ¼-inch slope on each tread for drainage. A bevel on the lower edge of the form will permit finishing the full tread width. Brace the forms well. Wood cleats are the best way to attach riser forms to

Wood float being used to rough-finish concrete. In background on ground is bull float, a wood float with a long handle.

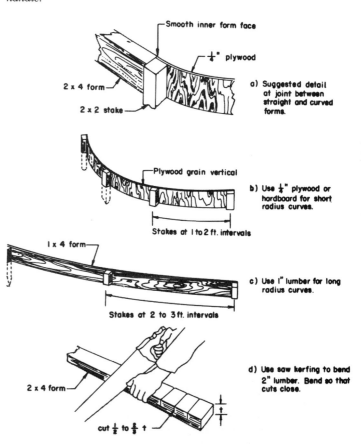

a) Suggested detail at joint between straight and curved forms.

b) Use ¼" plywood or hardboard for short radius curves.

c) Use 1" lumber for long radius curves.

d) Use saw kerfing to bend 2" lumber. Bend so that cuts close.

Four ways to create curved forms. Forms are good for any kind of flat concrete work — such as drives, patios, sidewalks.

plywood sidewall forms. Use wood wedges to hold risers between solid concrete or masonry walls. Braces are usually centered on the risers and staked and nailed in place.

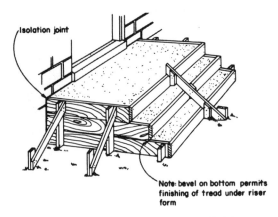

Forms for steps. Note expansion strip at wall. This prevents concrete from bonding to wall.

As you install riser forms, install them so the tread will pitch ¼ inch for drainage.

Another way to build forms. Risers are braced securely with nailed-on boards. Note wedges at concrete wall.

As you build forms, allow for any recesses needed for attachment of ironwork or railings. Also, an isolation joint is required where the top tread or landing meets the building. A thin layer of building paper will do the job. If this is not done, the concrete might bond to the wall and someday crack.

Fill Materials

Use the broken-up pieces of the old steps as "fill" for the new. This reduces the amount of concrete needed. But don't have any fill material any closer than 4 inches from the face of any form. You want solid concrete there.

You can use the same concrete mix for steps as you use for driveways, but the maximum size of coarse aggregate used should not exceed 1 inch.

Before pouring the concrete, wet the forms with water or oil. Forms to be removed the same day can be wetted with water; those that are to stay in place several days should be oiled.

Start pouring concrete into the bottom step form and work upward, filling against sidewall forms as the work progresses. Poke the concrete with a spade, especially next to form faces, to work it into the fill. Use a wood float to strike excess off each step as it is filled. Finally, tap forms lightly to release any trapped air bubbles.

Finishing Steps

There are a few ways to finish your steps. One good way is to start at the top step using an edger (¼- to ½-inch radius) to bevel the edge of the step. Then use a wood float to smooth it, and follow with a further smoothing with a trowel. Wait until the steps are set sufficiently to hold their shape, then remove riser boards. Float each riser, and use an inside step tool where the riser meets the tread below to indent cleanly. The radius of this tool is usually the same as that used at the top of the riser.

If sufficient smoothing cannot be accomplished, a little mortar consisting of one part cement to about 1½ parts fine sand should be applied and troweled. After troweling, draw a damp brush across the riser to get a fine-textured, nonslip surface. Repeat for each riser.

Fill material for forms. This shouldn't go any closer than 4 inches from forms.

Fast and careful work is essential since too much time on any one step may cause the others to set too firmly for proper finishing.

Remove side forms the same day, float them, then plaster with a ⅛- to ¼-inch layer of mortar. Spread the mortar with a trowel, then float it with a cork or sponge rubber float. This finish is suitable for most step sidewalls. If a smooth finish is desired, troweling with a steel trowel

After concrete has set, remove riser forms, then trowel.

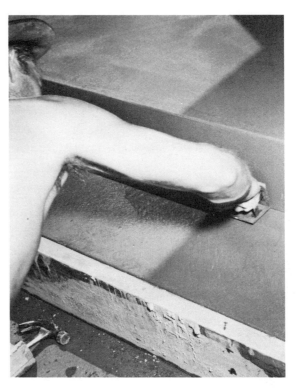

There is a special tool for finishing that lets you indent the steps cleanly.

should follow. After this, let the concrete cure properly by keeping it wet for a week.

Nonslip Finishes

Nonslip finishes for better safety on steps can be obtained in a number of ways. Brushing, swirl-floating, and swirl-troweling produce a rough texture, but these may wear smooth under heavy traffic. A more permanent nonslip tread can be gotten by using a dry-shake of abrasive grains such as silicon carbide or aluminum oxide. These are sprinkled on while the concrete is still wet. The most permanent nonslip steps are built with special abrasive strips and nosings that are embedded in the concrete.

One Step

If you have only one step that's beyond repair, your job is much easier. As with more than one step first use a sledgehammer to break up the step. Clean the area, then follow instructions below for building a new one.

You can install the step directly on firm

Form for a single step. Single step may be poured directly on firm earth.

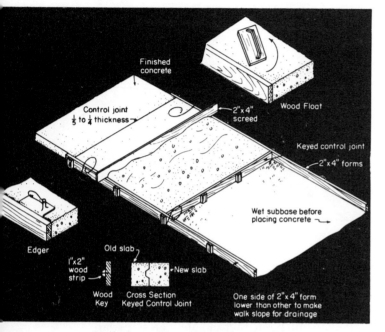

Methods used for making sidewalks. Control joints are created so that if concrete has a tendency to crack, it will crack internally at control joint and not be noticeable. On walks, figure a control joint for every four feet, or in increments according to walk width (for a 5-foot wide walk a control joint every 5 feet; 4-foot wide, every 4 feet; etc.).

earth. Use smooth 2 x 6 or 2 x 8 form boards, depending on height of step wanted. Form as shown in first sketch and brace well. Use carpenter's level for accuracy. Slope away from house at the rate of ⅛ inch per foot.

After pouring concrete (a premix is fine), tamp into place, rough level with a straight board or screed. To do this rest screed on form and move forward in a sawing motion. Round edges of step with edging tool.

A half-hour or more after screeding, as concrete begins to set, finish surface with wood float for a nonskid texture. (Use steel trowel for smooth finish.) Use a half-arc motion under light pressure. Re-edge with edging tool. Cure concrete by covering concrete with wet paper, burlap, or cloth the second day after pouring. Keep concrete damp for one week.

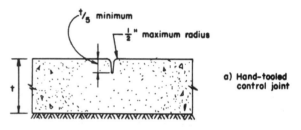

Closeup of control joint. This is made with a special tool designed for the purpose. Joints can also be power-sawed when concrete is hard.

7
Siding Solutions

Depending on what kind of siding you have on your home it will be more or less susceptible to damage. Wood siding develops cracks and can warp, asbestos siding, which is brittle, cracks, aluminum siding dents. No matter what the problem, it is usually within the scope of the beginner's skills to make the necessary repairs.

Asbestos Shingles

One of the problems with these shingles — in fact any kind of siding — is that the nails come loose. But making the repair is something that should be approached gingerly. As mentioned, this type of shingle is brittle, and can crack very easily.

If the nail is still there, gently tap it back in place almost flush. For the last half inch or so, use a nail-set — a thin, rodlike affair that looks like an oversized nail — to tap it in the rest of the way. This lessens your chances of giving the shingle an errant tap. A tap is all you need to break it. Just drive the nail flush, no more.

If there are no existing nails, or the ones you reset are still loose, use some extra nails. Drill small holes through the shingle, an inch or two from where the existing ones are, then set the new nails in. Nails should be an annular ring type and of galvanized steel or some other metal that doesn't rust.

Cracked Asbestos Shingle

If the shingle is cracked, but both pieces are in place, you needn't replace it. Just slide a sheet of roofing felt under the shingle (you will probably have to pull nails part way out first) so it's completely beneath the crack. Then drive new nails in at the bottom edge of the shingle, after drilling small holes for the nails first.

If a shingle is in really bad shape, then replacement is called for.

Shingles are nailed to the house at the top and bottom, with the top nails going through the bottom of the course above. To remove the shingle, you have a variety of methods at your disposal. Since shingles are brittle, you can simply

Asbestos shingle with common malady of this type shingle — it's cracked. Shingles of this type are most vulnerable when installed at the bottom of house. Here, the tarpaper is also ripped, and it must be replaced.

demolish the bad one in place with a hammer, taking care not to hit good ones, and remove it piece by piece. Another way is to slip a hacksaw blade between the shingle and overlapping course above and cut the nails; also cut nails at the bottom this way. Use pliers to remove pieces of nails.

One way to remove asbestos shingle is by slipping hacksaw under it and severing nails. Shingles are secured at both top and bottom.

To replace the shingle, simply slide it up in place so it is aligned with adjacent shingles and nail in place. Shingles come with predrilled holes. If you can align these with the ones on the other shingles, fine; if not, drill new ones.

Wood Shingles

Repairing wood shingles is similar to repairing asbestos ones.

First, hammer all nails in flush with the surface. If a shingle is cracked in one spot, you can insert a piece of roofing felt underneath, then nail the shingle tight at the bottom.

If the shingle requires replacement, nails, of course, must also be removed. Wood shingles are commonly nailed through the bottom and the top. Under the shingles at the bottom there may be strips of wood that raise them for a shadow effect.

To remove the nails you can insert a hacksaw blade under the shingle and cut the nails. Or, you can chisel a little space around the exposed nails to create a space for pulling the nails out with pliers. The latter method is slower, but will work if the hacksaw blade doesn't (sometimes shingles are nailed on so tight you can't slip the blade in). Then pry the shingle out, install the new one and nail in place. Ask your dealer about the best nails to use if you are uncertain.

Clapboard

Wood siding also comes in long-board form; if it is tapered at the top, it's called bevel siding. But if it is locked together at top and bottom, with one board fitting into the slots of the other (tongue and groove), it's called drop siding.

There is also a siding made up of "1-by" (1 x 8, 1 x 10, 1 x 12) made of boards that are not tapered at the top but are overlapped. This and bevel siding are often called clapboard.

If boards are slightly cracked, you can fill them with caulking compound or wood putty. The latter is a fibrous wood material that comes in paste form and is easy to apply with a putty knife. When dry, it can be sanded, sawed, or drilled just like wood. Work it into the cracks well with a putty knife.

Bad Cracks

If the clapboard siding or "1-by" is badly cracked or rotted, complete replacement is called for. If the particular length of clapboard is short, then you may be able to buy and replace it with a new board. However, if the board is long, then you can get by with a patch.

Clapboard is nailed at the bottom and the top. Top nails go through bottom of boards above.

The repair is made by cutting out the bad section with a backsaw, or small handsaw, and nailing a new piece in. To do this, first insert two tapered wedges an inch or so to either side of the bad section, and three-fourths up the width of the board — enough to create space beneath it and the board below. This will provide room for the saw to cut. If you wish, you can protect the boards beneath the bad one by wedging slim blocks of wood beneath your saw lines.

Take Out Nails

When you've cut through on both sides, drive the wedges a little higher, underneath the board above, and proceed to take out the bad section. Sometimes you can do this by hand; sometimes you will require a chisel and hammer. Take care not to tear tar paper if you're using a chisel.

If most of the piece breaks off, but some is left under the board above, slip a hacksaw up there and cut the nails out. If the whole piece comes out you can depress the board enough so you can grip the nail with a hammer and pull it out. You can then pry the strip out with a screwdriver.

Examine Building Paper

When the piece is out, examine the building paper. If it is cut or torn, patch it with a glob of roofing cement. If it is ripped rather extensively, use large headed galvanized nails to secure a patch made of building paper over it, and seal edges with roofing cement.

Carefully measure the gap you have to fill and cut a new piece of clapboard to fit as well as

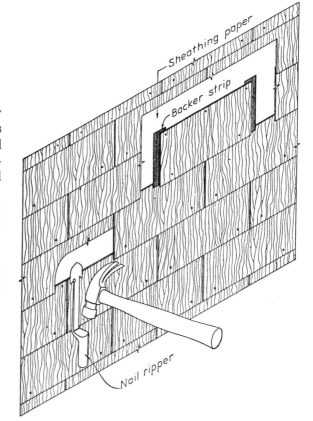

If you have a lot of shingles to remove, a nail ripper is a handy device. It slides under shingles; the hooked part grabs the nail; and you hammer on the bottom of the nail ripper to remove nail.

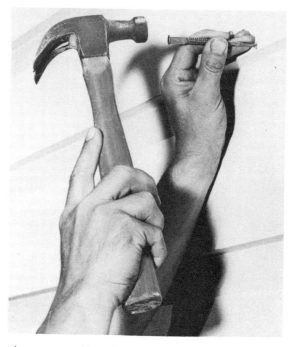

A common problem of all shingles is that the nails pop (come loose). Tap them back in place using a hammer and nailset.

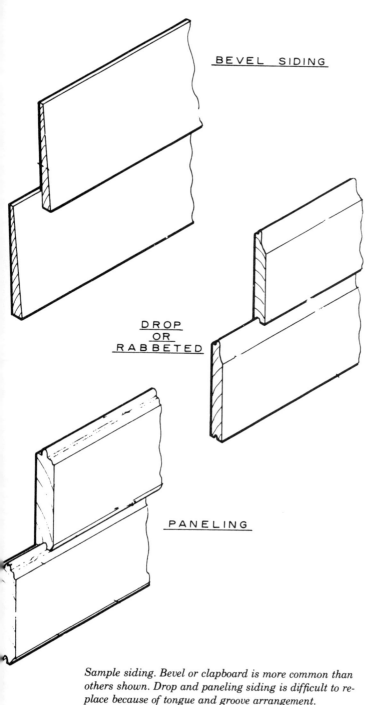

BEVEL SIDING

DROP
OR
RABBETED

PANELING

Sample siding. Bevel or clapboard is more common than others shown. Drop and paneling siding is difficult to replace because of tongue and groove arrangement.

possible. Place it under the board, then tap it in place with a hammer, using a block of wood as a cushion against denting the board edge. With the new piece in place, nail down permanently at top and bottom. If top board is old and dried out, it's best to drill pilot holes for the nails. Sink nail heads — you should use finishing nails — slightly below the surface and fill the depressions above with glazing compound or wood putty. Apply a prime coat of paint, then fill edges of patch with caulking compound and fill nail-head depressions with wood putty. A final coat of paint can then be applied. Assuming you're painting the entire house, the patch should blend in quite nicely.

Drop Siding

Drop siding, because of the way it is nailed, can only be broken out with a hammer and chisel, piece by piece. Then you cut a board to fit, first trimming the tongue off the top piece to make it fit in. But this makes for a difficult repair, and you'd be better off to try and patch the bad board with wood putty.

To replace clapboard, cut out bad part, then replace with cut section with square ends. Note the nailholes in existing clapboard; the new piece is secured on the top and bottom. Also caulk joints where patch meets adjacent siding.

8
Fixes for Furniture

Most outdoor furniture, at least pieces made of wood, is made to withstand rigorous use and battering by weather. But wood and pieces of other materials are susceptible to a variety of maladies. Wood tables warp, chair webbing splits or breaks, vinyl covers get stained or ripped. Repairs can be made to correct these problems relatively simply. Let's take a look at them.

Damaged Vinyl

In the old days, this repair was made with colored tape but today there are vinyl-repair kits that really do what they advertise — make the repair all but invisible.

All generally work the same way. First, you trim off the ragged edges of the rip or hole; or, in the case of a stain, cut it out neatly. Then, select one of the vinyl compounds in a color to match the existing vinyl. If one color doesn't do it, you mix a couple together to get the match. If the hole is small, you simply smear the colored compound over it. Then you select one of the graining papers — pieces of material with surfaces embossed or textured to match surfaces of a variety of vinyls. Press the appropriate graining sheet onto the compound, then apply heat with an iron for a minute or so. Peel back the graining sheet and there's the repair.

Damaged Aluminum

If the leg of an aluminum chair collapses, you don't need to relegate it to the scrap heap. You can make a splint for it, with the trick being that the splint is on the inside of the leg.

First, use a hacksaw to cut out the damaged section. Cut a piece of dowel about 4 inches longer than the piece you removed. (Drill a hole 2 inches in from each end of the dowel. Insert a nail in each hole, then slip the dowel into the cut ends of the tubing; the nails will space the dowel properly.)

Smear aluminum epoxy inside the ends and side of the dowel, and push it snugly in place. Pull nails and apply a thin coat of the compound to the portion of the dowel that remains exposed. When dry, use a file and sandpaper to

If webbing on a chair wears out, it can be bought in kits or you can make your own. Two-inch woven cotton (from upholstery stores) works well; or, for an even tougher chair seat, you can use 8-ounce canvas in 3-inch strips. Hem them ¼ inch to form 2-inch strips. To install, run strips one way (on underside of frame), then weave in other strips, folding all double at end, and fasten to chair with wood screws driven through small square cleats. (Cleats prevent webbing from tearing.)

smooth the rough edges of the aluminum compound.

Broken Webbing

If webbing on an outdoor chair is broken, it really doesn't pay to try and fix the broken pieces. Best bet is to replace all of it.

There are webbing kits available for this purpose with full installation instructions.

Canvas Chairs

If you find that a canvas material is pulling from the frame of a chair, resecure it by inserting No. 6 pan-head self-tapping screws — they make their own holes in metal — first installing a washer bent to conform to tubing shape under each screw.

If covers are torn, the simplest solution is simply to sew them closed. Making a reinforcing patch underneath the tear will give the patched area additional strength.

Redwood Furniture

Redwood is one of the hardiest woods of all, and doesn't require any protection from weather. Left alone, it will weather to a gray color. However, some people don't like this color, preferring a natural look. If so, or if your current

To give redwood furniture new life, apply a redwood stain, then finish with a protective coating of polyurethane.

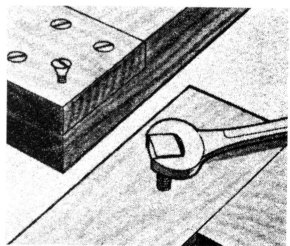

If furniture is wobbly, check for loose fasteners — screws or nails. Even if original fasteners were nails, you can use screws for extra strength.

furniture is gray and you'd like to give it new life, the answer is a redwood stain finish. There are many different brands of this and application is as easy as applying paint. Then to give it protection against staining from food and drink and weather, apply one of the clear polyurethane finishes.

Warped Tabletop

Tabletops that are particularly thin — less than 1 inch — have a tendency to warp. To protect against this problem you can obtain aluminum angles which you slip over each of the short ends of the table, then secure with aluminum nails or screws. It's best to drill pilot holes, small holes about half the length of the screw and of slightly smaller diameter, in the tabletop to prevent splitting the thin wood.

Furniture pieces that are joined by any kind of fasteners can also become loose. Consequently, the piece will wobble and may eventually collapse. The solution is simple. Search out the loose fasteners and tighten them up; or in the case of nails, remove and drive new ones. To guard against rust, use galvanized or aluminum fasteners.

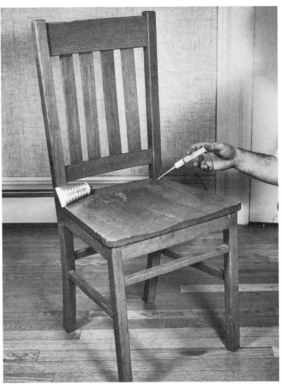

If piece is joined without fasteners (nails or screws) and it wobbles because joints are loose, you can get a product that swells wood and adheres it at the same time to make tighter joints. If you wish, apply it with a cheap plastic syringe, or swab it in place with a Q-tip.

Rusty metal furniture should be de-rusted (liquid removers work well), sanded smooth, and a primer and finish coat made for metal should be applied.

Metal furniture that develops loose or broken parts can be made like new with "Plastic Steel." A small jar of this material is shown on the floor in front of chair.

9
Pool Care

To insure season-long swimming fun, a minimal amount of time has to be devoted to the non-fun aspects of swimming pools — namely, the care and maintenance of the pool. It is a simple job if it is done properly and at the required intervals. It is when these routine tasks are neglected that trouble begins.

Need for Chemicals

One of the most important aspects of pool care is maintaining a proper chemical balance of the water. A glass of water coming out of the tap looks and (usually) tastes clean and clear. Put the same water in a 20 x 40 pool and it may have a different look entirely.

That's why you shouldn't use your pool the first day you fill it up, regardless of how tempting it is and how hot the weather. The first thing you should do is turn the filter on and let it run for a day. The filter will remove minerals and other solids that are present in most water. Any turgidity in the water should be removed, and the water should look sparkling clear after the first day.

From the very first day you fill your pool, its purity must be guarded by a chemical disinfectant. Some purifying agent — whether it be chlorine, bromine, or iodine — must be in there to kill disease-carrying bacteria brought into the water by bathers.

Chlorine is the most widely used disinfectant. It should be used at one part per million (ppm) ideally, and must have at least 0.6 ppm of "free residual chlorine." The actual ratio is really very small, since 100 percent activity is gained by only one drop of chlorine for every one million drops of water.

Routine Cleaning

In addition to keeping the proper chemical balance, there are a few other things that should be done to keep your pool water clean and fresh. Some of these are:

- Manually skim the pool's surface with a standard "leaf skimmer," a netlike pool-cleaning tool designed especially to rid the pool's surface of leaves, bugs, debris and other floating contaminants. Many leaf skimmers have plastic nets. Most are equipped with long handles to enable you to reach the pool's center while standing on the pool deck.
- Brush down walls and tile. For this you'll need a stiff-bristled "tile brush" to clean near the waterline and a "wall brush" to clean the walls below.
- Clean the skimmer's basket and the hair-lint strainer. No special equipment is needed for this. Remove the skimmer basket and the hair-lint strainer from the pump. Get rid of the debris that has collected there and replace them. This should be done as frequently as possible — daily is

It doesn't take much effort to keep a pool the way it should be — clean, cool, and inviting.

Like any concrete structure, concrete pools are subject to cracking. Chip cracks out with a chisel, then tamp in special patcher.

These repaired cracks indicate that this pool may be not too long for this world. The cracks follow a consistent pattern.

preferable — or even more often during the spring and fall when there is a heavy fallout from leaves and bushes. Failure to keep baskets clean will result in reduced circulation of the water through the pump and filter.

- Vacuum the pool bottom. You'll need a special pool vacuum for this. There are many models and types. Consult your dealer as to the types best suited to your pool.
- Clean the filter. A dirty filter will result in decreased recirculation and consequently in dirty water. Consult the manufacturer of the filter (directions will be supplied when new) for the correct procedure for your particular filter. Most likely you should "backwash," or reverse the flow of water.
- Hose the deck clean. A garden hose is all the equipment you'll need. This should be done during every pool-cleaning.

Painting

Many pool owners leave their pools unpainted, but paint does make a pool more attractive. The trouble with painting is that you'll have to repaint every few years.

There are two main points regarding pool painting. The first is to be sure to use alkali-resistant paints for concrete or Gunite (a special concrete). Second, make sure that the surface is prepared properly.

The first step in preparation is to remove the water and repair all cracked or damaged areas to present a smooth surface throughout. If the paint is just dull or rubbed off, a thorough scrubbing is all that is necessary. If there is peeling or flaking, it may be necessary to remove the old paint completely. If so, sandblasting is the best way. You can either rent the equipment or have professional sandblasters brought in for the job.

Winterizing

In most parts of North America, there are at least a few months of the year when the weather is too cold for swimming.

The most important thing to remember about winterizing pools is to leave the water in.

The water serves to brace the walls against pressures created by frozen or shifting earth on the outside of the walls.

Some of the other things you should do before shutting up for the winter are:

- Clean the pool thoroughly.
- Lower the water to below the inlet suction fitting.
- Remove lights.
- Drain all lines at lowest points.
- Insert rubber plugs tightly in all openings so that no water may enter.
- Fill pool again to within two inches of the bottom of the skimmer opening. Make certain that main drain valve is closed off.
- Add an extra heavy dose of chlorine.
- Spread pool cover if using one.
- Place all removed parts in a dry, warm place and properly oil, grease, or paint where necessary.
- Plug all lines so that vermin or mice cannot enter system.
- Remove diving board and store on edge.
- Disconnect all electrical energy.
- Stuff a semi-inflated bicycle tube into the skimmer to absorb pressures created by freezing and thawing.
- Check pool from time to time. If water has receded below the ice on top, refill with garden hose until water meets ice. Suspended ice can cause pool damage.

Hole in Pool

A minor miracle of technology, at least to me, is that today you can repair a hole in a vinyl-lined pool even under water. There are repair kits consisting, basically, of patches and adhesive that "melts" the vinyl and fuses the patch to it.

To make an above-water repair, first clean the area to be patched to remove algae, soil, pool chemicals, and the like. Then cut the patch to the shape needed, apply adhesive to the back, and set it firmly in place. If the area cut is puckered, you should flatten it out first (strips of tape help) before applying the patch.

For an underwater repair, first cut the patch to shape needed. Apply an extra heavy coat of adhesive. Go under the water and wipe the patch clean as well as you can with a rag. Then dive again and press the patch firmly in place. That's it.

Correcting Water Discoloration

Discoloration of pool water can stem from a number of causes. Here are some of the causes and how to correct them.

Algae can turn water greenish and cloudy. To restore your pool to its natural sky-blue color, treat the water with the proper amount of disinfectant and an algicide. Certain algicides may cause a very fine hazy cloudiness temporarily in some water.

Red-Brown Water: The addition of disinfectants may oxidize the iron in water. Since oxidized iron is insoluble, rust particles give the water a reddish brown color. To correct, filter continuously for about 48 hours. At the same time, add even more of the oxidizing sanitizer. It will oxidize any remaining dissolved iron in the water. Particles not removed by the filter will settle to the pool bottom, where they should be removed with the pool vacuum as soon as they show up to prevent staining.

Cloudiness: Winds — carrying algae spores, dust, and debris — can cause the water to turn cloudy. Windblown debris may, on occasion, also change pool water's balance — its pH or alkalinity. To correct, adjust the sanitizer level and pH balance to remove the dirt, and clean the filter as needed.

pH too high: One form of cloudiness is caused by excessively high pH, which causes the precipitation of insoluble salts. This cloudiness may not be too apparent during the daytime, but shows up as a haziness in the water at night when underwater lights are on. Correction is easily made by restoring the water's proper pH balance (adding acid to bring the water's balance to 7.2 to 7.6 pH).

10
Roof Repair

When you think about it, your roof takes more abuse than any other part of the house. The sun beats down on it, rain lashes it, snow settles on it, wind whips it. Roofs are built to last, but any damage they sustain should be promptly corrected.

In general, repairing most types of roofing is fairly easy. But it is not something to attempt if height makes you queasy. No need to have to get yourself repaired. At any rate, you should wear sneakers or no shoes and only work on a nice, relatively wind-free day.

Safety Ladders

A good number of outdoor repairs — on gutters, roofs, high windows, for example — will require the use of a ladder. Today, the range of ladder designs, types, sizes, and materials is broad enough to fit your particular needs.

In laying roofing or in making repairs, a long wooden ladder or a so-called chicken ladder may be used for safety. The chicken ladder is made by nailing 1- x 2-inch cleats about a foot apart on a 1- x 10-inch plank or similar long board. Either type of ladder may be hooked over the ridge of the roof, as shown in the sketches. Hooks are made by nailing a strong piece of wood to each leg near the upper end of the ladder at an angle with the legs. This angle should conform as nearly as possible to the slope of the roof, and the pieces which form the hooks should be braced or stiffened by nailing short boards between them and the legs of the ladder.

Asphalt Shingles

The most common kind of roofing is asphalt shingles — the kind with the granular surface.

One of the more common problems is that the shingles crack. If so, you can use roofing cement and a trowel and fill the crack with the material. This material expands and contracts with weather — it won't crack like roofing tar. If you get the roofing cement on shingles, wipe it away with a kerosene-soaked rag. The material is black, so will show up against a light-colored roofing.

Popped Nails

Another problem with asphalt shingles is popped nails. This is usually caused by strong winds: They lift the shingle, taking the nail right with it. If installing a new roof, incidentally, consider installing shingles with adhesive tabs — they can withstand hurricane-force winds. The solution is simple. Use new galvanized or aluminum nails to hammer it in place. Nails should only be flush with the shingle surface, not below. Or, you can adhere it with a couple of globs of roofing cement. Cover the heads of new nails and old holes with roofing cement to prevent water penetration.

Replacing Shingles

Shingles may also require replacement. For example, the granular material may have worn away — look for dark gray or black patches which signal this; you may also find the granular material washed into gutters. Or, pieces of shingle may have been lifted off by wind, or they may be cupped (curled at edges) or very badly split. Heavy rains or wind can finish these shingles off.

A hot day when shingles are pliable is the best time to do any shingle repair work.

If the shingle is on the body of the house, it will be nailed in place in the middle. Just lift the shingle and pry the nails loose with a pry bar, and slip the shingle out. Secure the new shingle with 1½-inch roofing nails, placing the nails in the same pattern used when removing the bad shingle. The standard method of nailing is shown in the sketch.

You may find that the shingle is secured by additional nails at the top edge, securing the overlapping shingle. In this case, remove your first set of nails from the middle of the shingle. If you can lift the shingle above to get at the top nails, fine. If not, pull the shingle straight out, ripping it free from the nails. Use the damaged shingle as a pattern and cut small cut-outs in the top edge of the replacement shingle where the old nails were. Then simply slide the new strip in place: The cut-outs will let you do this without the top nails interfering. Then, secure it with nails as high up as you can place them, and use roofing cement under the flaps as extra security.

Two types of scaffolding that can be used for roof repair. Chicken ladder is made by nailing cleats to plank; ladder at right is regular rung ladder. Both ladders attach to roof by means of "hook" arrangement at roof peak.

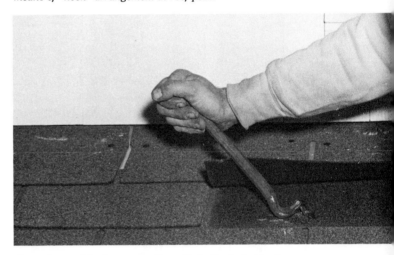

To replace a shingle, remove the nails in the bad shingle and in the one above it.

Shingle will be easier to work with on a warm day. With nails removed, it should slide out easily.

Re-nail shingle using roofing nails. Use the pattern of nailing that you observed when taking the old shingle out.

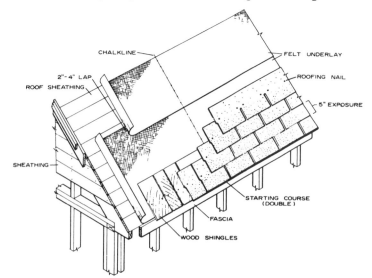

Standard method of nailing shingles on.

If you get roofing cement on shingle, remove the cement with kerosene.

If the shingles are damaged down at the edge of the house, you may have to put in a so-called starter course before nailing on a new shingle. The starter course, commonly 7 inches wide, is shown in the sketch.

Replacing Ridge or Hip Shingles

Shingles that are located along the ridge, or spine, of the house or the hip may also need replacement. Here, you may be able to use the damaged shingle as a pattern for cutting the new one. Or, remove a good shingle and use that. Nail in place following nail placement used on the other shingles.

Wood Shingles

This is another fairly common kind of roofing material. One problem these shingles develop is splitting. This type of shingle is rigid and you can't easily lift it to remove the nails securing it. So demolish it in place — break it up into pieces — with a hammer or small ax, being careful not to damage other shingles. Then, slip a hacksaw blade under the shingle where it's nailed and saw the nails flush with the surface, or as close to the surface as you can get.

Cut a shingle to the width needed. Slide in place, until its edges are aligned with adjacent shingles. Drive a nail in the middle of the shingle, then cover the head with a dot of roofing cement. Whether you use one or more shingles, they should be placed so that the joints between them or adjacent shingles do not coincide with shingle joints above or below.

Replacing Shingles in More Than One Course

If you find that shingles in a number of courses need replacement, follow this procedure. Split up and pull out damaged shingles in the uppermost row and hacksaw off nails. This then will make it easy to remove damaged shingles in rows below.

When the area is clear, start securing new shingles, following nailing pattern observed when you removed the damaged ones, except for the top row: Face nail these in place, covering nail heads with dabs of roofing cement.

Any patch will stand out on the roof but trying to stain them to match existing roofing isn't easy. It's usually better to let them weather naturally. Eventually their appearance will catch up with the rest of the roof.

Slate and Tile

Tile and slate roofs are very durable indeed, but they can develop cracks. To repair these, you can use roof cement, wiping up any mess with kerosene. Replacing either type is really a job for a professional.

Built-up Roofing

This is one of the easiest kinds of roofing to repair, because it's laid relatively flat. You can walk around on it without having to be careful of your balance.

One problem is that the roofing curls up at the edges. Use a brush to clean out accumulated debris under the edge. Spread a roofing cement under the curled-up edge, then nail it down securely with large head nails. Apply roofing cement over the edge and on nail heads.

Splits

If the roofing is split, use a utility knife to cut away all ragged edges. Spread roof cement over the spot and 2 inches to all sides. Put a piece of asbestos-saturated felt and press tightly into the cement, then nail in place. Apply more cement along the edges, and over nails. Sprinkle a little gravel over the patch for protection against weathering.

Flashing Repair

Flashing is the thin, fairly pliable material used on roofs to seal gaps between the roofing material and other materials, such as between roofing and a chimney, between roofing sections such as in the valleys of a house, or between siding and roofing.

One problem is rust. This can form and even-

Hip or ridge shingles may require replacement. Here you cut part of a regular shingle to pattern of damaged hip or ridge shingle. (Ridge shingles run along top of house; hip type run along tops of sloping parts.)

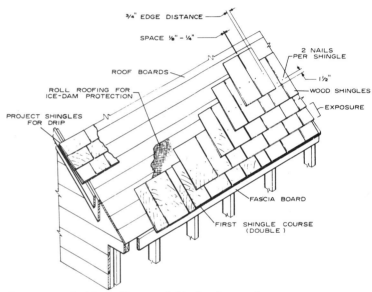
Common method for nailing wood shingles. See text for removal method.

Tile roof repair is a difficult job even for a professional. The material is too rigid to work with easily.

Built-up roofing is easy to repair because it's flat. On split, cut away ragged portion, then trowel on roofing cement.

Nail on a patch of asbestos felt, then apply roof-cement to edges and nails. As last step, sprinkle a little gravel over the patch.

tually eat through the metal. Water then has free passage to the interior of the house.

If you see rust, use a wire brush to remove it and apply good metal paint. If there is a small hole, patch it with roofing cement. If the hole is large, obtain a piece of flashing, cut out a patch, and secure it with roofing cement. Make sure water can't get in under the edges.

Gaps

Also, check for gaps at flashing. One vulnerable spot is where overlap flashing exists. If there are gaps, plug them up with butyl rubber caulking compound. Another vulnerable spot is where the flashing meets the chimney. It commonly has a cap flashing which is bent over and stuck into the mortar. When this mortar crumbles, the flashing can get loose and water running down the chimney can get behind it.

You can replace the mortar with fresh mortar, resecuring the edge of the flashing, but a better method is to plug it up with a caulk. This has a much better chance of sticking. Before doing this, force the metal into its slots in the mortar as firmly as possible.

Vent Pipes

One other particularly vulnerable spot for leaks in a roof is the plumbing vent pipes. The point where they disappear into the roof is commonly covered with a metal or plastic collar with lips, or flanges, that extend under the shingles. The top of this preformed piece is usually caulked where it meets the pipe, and this caulk works loose or dries out. The answer is to apply fresh caulk (remove all crumbly or dried out material first). Roofing cement is equally as good if you have it on hand.

Finding a Roof Leak

Sometimes, one can make all obvious repairs on a roof in an attempt to stop a leak, and the leak persists. Where do you go from there?

To find the part of the roof that is leaking can be quite sneaky, because water flows, and the source of the leak can be far from where you notice the water. For example, water can enter at the top of a house, run along sheathing, then down onto roof rafters, run a little farther there, then run along the backside of plasterboard and be 10 or 15 feet from where it entered.

To find it, you need a hose and a helper. Stand on the roof directly above where the water is showing up inside. Someone should be stationed inside, directly below the spot. Turn

Vent pipe is particularly vulnerable to leaks. Apply caulk or roof-cement all around area shown.

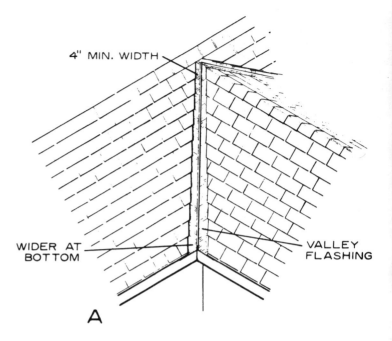

A

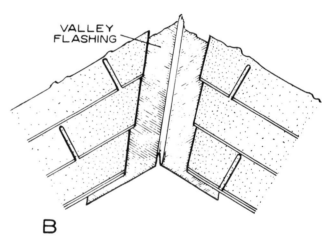

B

Two views of flashing, the material that bridges the gap between various materials (such as between roofing). (A) Valley flashing. (B) Note how flashing goes under shingles. It should be sealed underneath where it meets shingles.

on the hose and start running the water over that spot. Keep the water trained on the spot for a few minutes. If water appears inside, the helper should yell. If not, keep moving up the roof, repeating the procedure until you eventually find the leak.

Examine Area

Examine the area closely. If you see the source of the leak, plug it up. If not, remove shingles, including the felt beneath them, over a large enough area so that you're sure to uncover the source. Then install new felt and shingles.

Is It Worth Repairing?

While we've been talking about roof repair, some roofs may not really be worth the trouble — they're so far gone that only a new roof will do. If asphalt shingles are in generally bad shape, replacement is likely called for. However, there are treatments available that may give the roof a few years more life.

Professionals apply preservatives to wood and solvents or paint to asphalt. Usually, the pros will guarantee their work (if they don't, forget them) so they'll be inclined to tell you truthfully if the treatment is worthwhile, or if a new roof is called for. Incidentally, if having a paint job, you might want to consider one of the lighter colors, which reflect sunlight — heat — and can make a house much cooler in summer.

A New Roof

If you have to have a new roof, you can do the job yourself, but you have to be fairly handy.

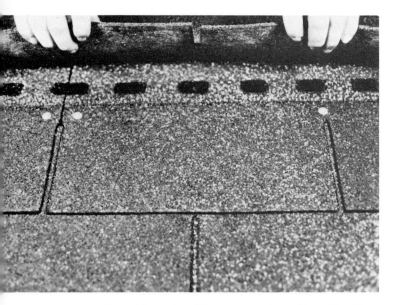

If considering installing a new roof, consider self-sealing type (black spots are adhesive). It can withstand hurricane-force winds.

New asphalt shingle job. It is usually okay to apply new roofing over existing one.

Sometimes, replacing a roof means going down to "deck" or roof sheathing and repairing it. All rotted or broken boards must go.

Manufacturers supply instructions with bundles of shingles. The roofing can go right over the existing roof, as long as it's the original roof. More than two layers of roofing weighs too much. Consider getting a heavyweight shingle if asphalt is your choice. These weigh from 265 to 385 pounds per square (10 x 10 square feet of roofing), come in various colors and textures, and are guaranteed to last 25 years. The average roof lasts 15 years.

11
Repairing and Replacing Screening

Screening is fairly delicate stuff, and it's the rare home indeed that can go an entire summer without one or more being damaged. Two types of screening are common — aluminum and plastic. What you do to correct the damage depends on which type you have, and the degree of damage.

Small Holes in Metal Screens

Some holes in metal screens aren't really holes, but simply screen wires that are pushed far enough apart to form a hole. If close inspection reveals this is the problem, simply take an awl, nail, or other sharply pointed item and push the wires back into correct position.

If there actually is a hole, but it is very small, you can sometimes fill it by squirting a blob of clear glue over it, effectively filling it.

Larger Holes

If the hole is too large for this kind of treatment, a patch is the answer. If you want to save a little money, and have some scrap screening handy, cut a square patch with a utility knife or tin snips, then sew the patch over the hole with individual strands of screen wire. Easier, though, is to buy a small package of patches at a hardware store. These come with hooked edges and are simple to install. You just position the patch over the hole, bend it slightly and locate so the hooked edges are threaded into the screening, and let go. It snaps in place.

Replace Screening

If the hole is too large to be handled by a patch, your best bet is to replace the screening.

Kits for the job, containing screening and hardware, are available, but this is not the way to go to save money. Less costly is to buy the screening loose. Hardware stores carry rolls of it — they'll cut off whatever size piece you need. You'll also need one basic tool. It has a handle with a convex wheel attached to one end, and a concave wheel on the other. At around 20¢ a square foot for

Sometimes a hole in screening isn't a hole — but is simply pushed-apart screen wires. To repair, simply realign them.

Actual small holes can be plugged with a small blob of household adhesive.

A hole this size is a candidate for a small patch. These come with hooked edges and are "snapped" in place.

screening, and $3 or $4 for the tool, replacing one screen is still cheaper than a kit or getting it done professionally.

First, remove the old screening. On metal frames, it is commonly held on by rubber or plastic strips, called spline, which wedges it down into grooves. Pry one end of the spline up with a screwdriver or knife tip. Once you can grab it, carefully, so as not to break it, pull it free. It may be in one piece or there may be separate pieces on each of the four frame sides.

Examine the spline. If it is not corroded or brittle, you may be able to use it for installing the new screening. If it is, get new spline. Since it comes in various sizes, your best bet is to show the dealer the old spline.

Cut Screening

Cut a piece of screening an inch larger all around than the frame. Set it squarely on the frame and smooth it flat. Clamp it on with two C clamps on any side. Begin working on the side opposite that. Using the concave wheel on the screening tool, make short back and forth

No patch is going to cure a problem this large — replacement of screening is necessary.

To replace metal screening that is held by a flexible spline in metal frame, first pry up one corner of spline and grab.

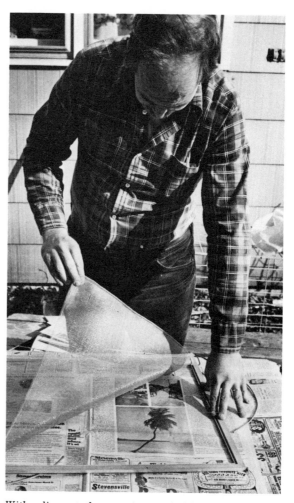

With spline out, the screening can be lifted out easily.

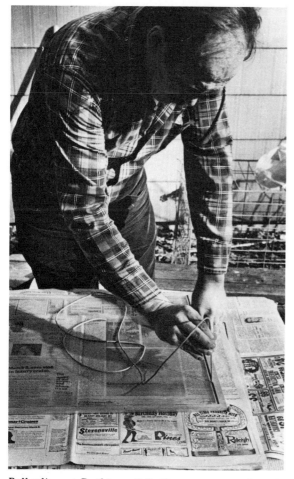

Pull spline out. Do this carefully if you expect to use it again.

Use small C clamps to clamp screen down on one side.

Use concave wheel on tool to force screening into groove on side opposite clamped side. Pull it taut as you do.

Then use convex wheel to force spline over screening. By this time screening should be tight across frame. Use short strokes to avoid tearing screen.

strokes to force the screening into the groove — don't try to force it down with one pass. As you do, use your free hand to pull it tight across the frame.

Inserting Spline

When a professional installs screening, he uses one long uncut spline piece, working it down into side after side, and rounding corners with ease. For the beginner, though, the best bet is to cut the spline into a separate piece for each side.

Place the spline against any side of the frame and cut it to the length needed.

Lay the spline over the groove, then use the convex wheel on the roller to work it snugly in place. Start from any end and work your way to the other end, using short strokes. To make the

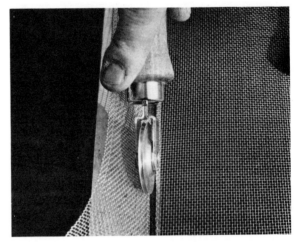

Closeup of convex wheel in action.

spline pliable — easier to work with — first wash it in warm soapy water.

Secure Opposite Side

With the screen secured on one side, go to the opposite side. Remove the C clamps, and repeat the procedure used on the first side. Then do the remaining two sides as you did the first two.

Finally trim excess screening. Use a sharp utility knife, or razor blade, holding it at an

Lay spline against groove, and cut to length.

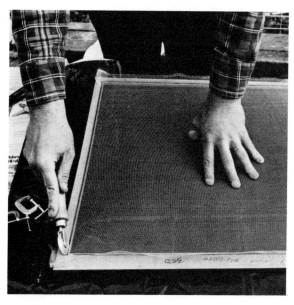

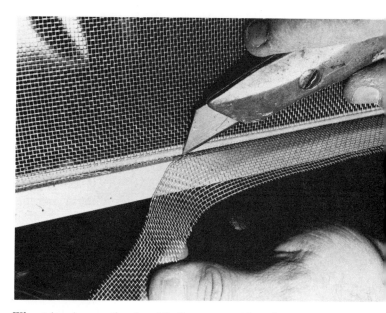

Proceed to opposite side, and follow the same procedure. Clamp another side, and do the same, then do the last side. Remember to pull screening tight across frame as you do.

When trimming, use the edge of the frame as a guide and cut toward outermost edge of frame.

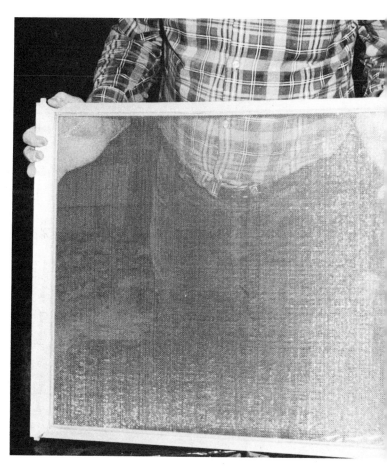

When all sides are done, trim excess screening with a sharp utility knife.

angle to the edge of the frame, and using the frame as a guide.

Some metal screens in metal frames are secured with rigid strips of metal rather than flexible spline. Here, you first remove the spline carefully with a screwdriver. Try not to bend it as you do. If it does bend you'll have to straighten it out before reinserting it.

Then, proceed as above to replace the screen. To get each strip back into its groove, gently tap along its length using a narrow wedge-shaped board and hammer.

Completed screen.

Metal Screening in Wood Frame

If you have the older type wood frame screens, installation depends on the way the screening is held on. If the frame is the type with a spline in a groove, you can proceed as for metal-frame screen. If you have the type where the screening edges are stapled or tacked to recesses all around the screen, and the edges are covered with a thin molding, proceed as follows: Gently pry the molding loose and unfasten the screen. Square a piece of screening as large as the frame over the frame. Fasten the screening to any side with C clamps. On the opposite side, pull the screening taut and staple it on, using a staple every 2 inches. Trim excess with a utility knife. One side done, release the other side, and staple this in place. Repeat procedure for the remaining two sides.

Metal screening in wood frame is stapled on (a staple every 2 inches or so); molding covers the edge of screening.

Fiberglass Screening

Repair of fiberglass screens is slightly different than for metal. For one thing, the fiberglass strands don't pull apart — they're fused together. But holes are as common as those in aluminum.

For small or fairly large holes, you can use a homemade fiberglass patch. Cut a piece of screening about a ¼ inch larger all around than the hole. Secure over the hole with a bit of plastic adhesive and the job's done.

If the hole is extra large, it's best to replace the entire screen. As with metal screens, the "how to" depends on the type of frame. If it is metal with a flexible spline, proceed as follows.

First, remove the spline. Place a piece of screening, about the same size as the frame over the frame. Clamp down any side. On the opposite side, pull the screening taut. Use your roller to wedge the screen and the spline into the groove simultaneously. Trim excess. Repeat the procedure on the other sides, trimming excess screening as you go. If the spline is rigid, proceed the same way, only use a wedge-shaped board and hammer to get the spline in place.

Wood Frames

If you have wood frames with a flexible spline, you can follow the same procedure as for metal frames. If the screening is tacked to recesses on frame, follow this procedure.

Place a frame-size piece of screening on the frame. Clamp one side. On the other, fold the edge of the screening over into a sort of hem and, as you pull it taut, staple it down, setting staples 2 inches apart. Loosen clamps and repeat procedure on opposite side, then do the other two sides. Replace molding.

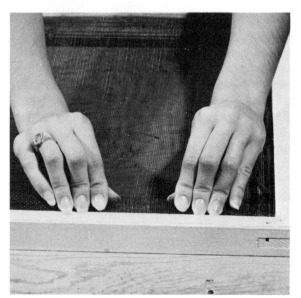

Fiberglass screening in a wood frame is doubled over at the edge, then . . .

. . . stapled on.

Painting Screens

Metal door and window screens will last longer — and look better — if they are kept well painted. For this, you can get special thin screen paints that won't clog the mesh. (Tip: A coat of thinned white paint applied to the screen wire makes the interior of the house less visible from the outside.)

How Often?

Frequency of painting depends on screen quality. A cheap grade will probably require painting every year, while galvanized screening may show signs of rust only after a long time and may then require only a light coat of paint. Copper or bronze screen wire will not deteriorate if not painted, but corrosion from weathering makes it advisable to paint or varnish copper or bronze screens to avoid them staining the trim and siding. If you want the original copper or bronze screen color, use a high-grade spar varnish. Apply two coats to each side of the screening. This will not last as long as the enamel, so you will have to coat them with spar varnish each season. If you have no objection to a dark color, a coat of thin black enamel should last several seasons.

Paint can be applied to screens evenly and economically with a special screen applicator. Most paint dealers carry these applicators, but, if not available, they are not hard to make. Cover a block of wood 1 x 3 x 8 inches with thick felt or carpet attached to the face side of the block with the fiber out. Nail a cleat of wood for a handle along the center of the opposite side of the block. Carpet may be fastened by glue or tacks, but if tacks are used, the heads should be well embedded so that they will not catch on the wire mesh when the paint is applied.

Place Screen Flat

The screen should be placed on a level surface like a table, then cleaned of all dust, soot, and loose rust with a bristle brush. If more thorough cleaning is necessary, wash the screen with soap and warm water (apply with a brush), then rinse with clear water, and dry with a cloth. After the screen has been cleaned on both sides and dried thoroughly, rub paint on, using small amounts of paint at one time, avoiding clogging the mesh.

Frames should not require painting more than once every 3 to 5 years. If the screens are cleaned and painted as described, their life will be prolonged and they will look better.

12
Face-lifts for Patio Slabs

Concrete is a great building material and can be molded into a great variety of dramatic, beautiful, and unique shapes. But in the form it exists in as a patio — a slab — it simply isn't going to win any beauty contests.

This needn't be the case. Today there is a wide variety of materials you can use to color or cover your patio and give it a whole new look. Following is a roundup of these products and tips on how they're installed so you can get an idea what will be best for you.

Seamless Flooring

This material gets its name from the fact that it has no seams, like paint. Indeed, application is similar and just about as easy.

First step is to clean the patio, and patch all cracks (see Chapter 5). Next, roll on a white base coat using a roller with an extension handle. While still wet, sprinkle colored vinyl chips, like confetti, onto this base coat. These form pattern and color. The chips are available in a wide variety of colors — and you can combine them — for interesting effect. A variation of the system is sprinkling colored sand on the base coat. Then, a coat of clear sealer is applied, allowed to dry and another coat of sealer is applied. When this dries, the job is done.

We applied one brand of this material in a kitchen (it's for indoor use as well) a few years ago and it worked fine, except that keeping it clean was difficult. It has a nubby texture, and dirt worked its way in all too well and merely mopping didn't get the dirt out. Scrubbing was the only solution. One manufacturer, Dur-A-Flex (100 East Meadow Street, Hartford, Connecticut 06114), says that this was because the clear sealer used was an acrylic plastic, rather than a urethane, which their system uses. Acrylic scratches more easily, they say, and dirt embeds itself in the scratches. At any rate, in an outdoor application, with constant washing by rain and with less traffic, maintenance should not be a big problem.

Before applying seamless flooring, slab must be patched. Here, fiberglass and compound is used to seal joint between slab and wall.

Partially finished patio. At left is white base-coat. Vinyl chips have been sprinkled on the right side. Following this, clear sealer-coat is applied.

Carpeting

Outdoor carpeting is now available in a wide variety of colors and styles and in sheet or tile form.

For the do-it-yourselfer, installing the tiles is easiest. Tiles come in 1-foot squares and may be installed on any clean, dry surface using plenty of adhesive as instructed by the manufacturer. Carpeting in sheet form is usually 12 feet wide and comes in a variety of lengths and in precut sizes, such as 9 x 12 feet. Sheet carpeting is also a relatively easy do-it-yourself job. Its one advantage over tiles is that it has fewer seams — dirt has less chance to collect.

You needn't cover an entire slab with carpeting. For example, a precut size can look nice in the center of the patio with the perimeters left uncovered — or covered some other way.

Carpet That Imitates Grass

An offbeat but popular sheet carpeting is a type that simulates grass. Some people like to install this as an accent material — around a pool or the like — while others will cover an entire area with it.

One buying tip: Read the guarantee carefully. While most carpeting will wear well for a long time, many will fade. Some companies guarantee against fading for five years, some do not for any time.

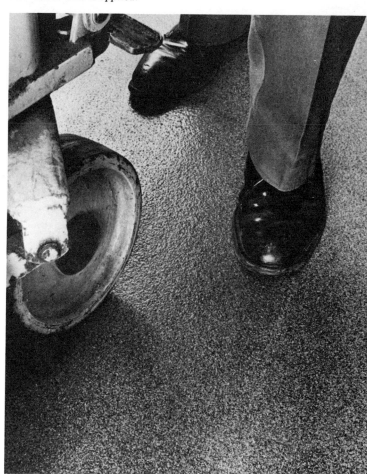

Closeup of seamless flooring shows its nubby texture. The material can withstand great weight and is highly resistant to cracking.

Here, outdoor carpeting is segmented by redwood strips for interesting effect on freeform patio.

Resilient Flooring

This material gives, or yields, when you step on it, hence its name. It has long been a mainstay flooring inside the house, but only recently has gone outside.

We know of only one manufacturer of the material now: National Floor Products of Florence, Alabama. Their material is made of vinyl resins and "colorfast" (manufacturer's claim) pigments with a backing of fiberglass asbestos. Installation, like carpeting, is with adhesive (epoxy). There is also a special adhesive used to fuse the seams so moisture can't get under the material.

Designs, as of this writing, were mostly confined to brick patterns — herringbone and side-by-side patterns. Both are textured to resemble real brick and joints are made of a "vinyl sand" that resembles mortar. The flooring is available in white and various brick colors and in 6-foot-wide sheets of continuous length.

Another style of carpeting has bright-colored stripes. Material can be installed by do-it-yourselfer.

Ozite's Lawnscape carpeting imitates and acts like grass, except for one prime difference: you don't have to cut it.

You're probably familiar with resilient flooring from its many indoor uses, but a sheet type in 6-foot widths and continuous lengths is available.

Resilient flooring is available in patterns resembling brick, with joints of a vinyl sand to resemble mortar.

Two-component epoxies are best. Mix them together just before use.

Paint

This is one of the old, old standbys for giving new life to a patio. There are three kinds generally used: latex, oil-base, and epoxy. Each has advantages and disadvantages.

Latex paints stand up to wear pretty well, but not as well as the oil-base types. However, the latex type has a low sheen while oil-base has a high gloss; latex will give you a less slippery surface when wet.

Epoxy is undoubtedly the best of the three paints — and the most expensive. The two component types — you mix them together before use — are usually better than the single can variety. It gives a hard, durable surface that will last indefinitely.

Different Colors

Floor paints are available in a wide variety of colors, and may be bought white and tinted to suit. Before applying any paint, patch all cracks, and clean the surface thoroughly, being especially alert for grease.

You can apply any of the paints with either a brush or roller. Most people find the roller and

a long-handled extension easiest — hardly any bending is necessary. Also, as with any paint, read the label before you start laying it on.

Staining and Dyeing Concrete

A slab can also be dressed up by staining or dyeing. Various products are available. Usually, they come in powder form which you mix with water, then apply with either brush or roller.

Spalled Concrete

Your slab may not only suffer from the blahs, looks-wise, but be spalled — a thin skin of concrete is virtually peeling from the surface. Spalling can be caused by a variety of things, including improper installation, but the only real solution is to remove all peeling layers of concrete and to apply some sort of material over it.

Cement is one answer. You can apply a coat of sand mix, an inch or two thick; this can be colored by adding powdered colorants to the mix or sprinkling the colorant on the surface after the cement is smoothed, but still wet.

Another coating is a sand-cement-epoxy

Paint application is easier with the roller attached to an extension handle, making getting down on hands and knees unnecessary.

Sand-cement-epoxy mixture can be troweled onto patio and is a good answer for slab that is badly damaged.

mixture. Dur-A-Flex is one manufacturer. The epoxy and aggregate (sand-cement) come in two separate cans which you mix together before use, and apply with a trowel, as thickly or thinly as required to create a smooth surface. You can use the floor the next morning (unlike mortar) and its colorful surface will resist most chemicals, oil, grease — just about anything. For easier cleaning, you can give the floor a coat of clear urethane, but this somewhat lessens its nonskid virtue.

Before applying the epoxy, though, it is necessary to remove all loose material with a hammer and chisel or other tool.

Even a patio as badly spalled as this can be face-lifted by sand-cement-epoxy mixture. Be very sure to get all scaling pieces off.

A flagstone patio that is in need of a new look can be dressed up nicely by painting the stones different colors.

View of slab after it has been face-lifted with sand-cement-epoxy mixture — a far cry from its previous condition.

. . . then tamped down solidly. Final treatment is application of another type of glaze on top. Surface is too rough for patio use. Dur-A-Flex makes glazes.

If your driveway has seen better days, one solution is shown here: Gravel mixed with a special binding glaze and troweled on . . .

13
Preseason Checkup
for a Lawn Mower

Just before you roll out your old power mower to take the turf down a few pegs is an excellent time to give it some tender loving care. This can save you a lot of headaches and repairs later.

Remove Spark Plug

Before working on the machine, it's a good idea to remove the spark plug. In this way accidental starting of the machine will be impossible.

The best tool for doing this is a spark plug wrench. They're sold at hardware and auto supply stores. They let you get a good grip on the plug and turn it out easily.

Empty Old Fuel

Any fuel — gas and oil — from last season should be discarded. This and other operations should be done in a well-ventilated area. To empty gas, simply tip the machine and empty it into a large container. A flat wide pan is usually handy for catching old oil. Let it drain awhile to get out as much of the oil as possible.

While you've got it out, the spark plug should be cleaned and gapped — the distance between the bent-over metal part on top and the spark plug proper adjusted. To clean, rub the plug and metal part with a piece of fine emery cloth (available at hardware stores).

To gap the plug, obtain a gapping tool at hardware stores and measure the distance. If too short (see your operator's manual), bend the terminal upward until it's right; if too big, bend downward. For better contact when reinstalling the plug, coat the screw threads on it with graphite grease.

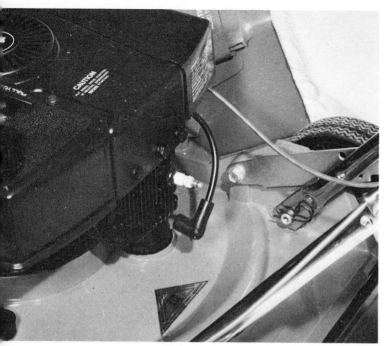

Before doing any work on mower, remove spark-plug wire by grasping it at the fat part (not by the wire) and pulling out. In photo, wire hangs free from plug.

Empty all gas and oil from last season. A flat pan is useful for draining oil. Let machine drain awhile to remove as much oil as possible.

Cleaning Machine

The mower may still be laden with grass clippings, dirt, and other debris from last year. Rust may also be evident.

To clean, turn the machine on its side, or over completely. Use a screwdriver, paint scraper, or wire brush to clean the machine. Pay special attention to the cooling fins on the motor — clogged ones can affect engine performance. If there is rust, remove this with the wire brush or rust-remover liquid, rinse clean, and spray a rust-inhibiting paint on the area.

Adjust Carburetor

Over a season, a lawn mower vibrates like a milkshake mixer, and thus the carburetor can be knocked out of adjustment. Check your operator's manual and reset it. After you've run it awhile, you may have to readjust it for smoother operation. Vibration also affects nuts and bolts, so tighten all that you see.

Clean Air Filter

Lawn mowers have an air filter which must be periodically cleaned or replaced. Your operator's manual will indicate its location and cleaning requirements. On some mowers, you wash the filter in detergent, then squeeze it dry; the element on it should be coated with oil and the excess squeezed out. Also, use a soft brush to clean the area around the filter. Some filters have a paper element that requires replacing. Your dealer should have one.

Blade Sharpening

It is important to have a sharp set of blades on a mower. Dull ones can bruise grass and make it turn brown. This is something your dealer can take care of.

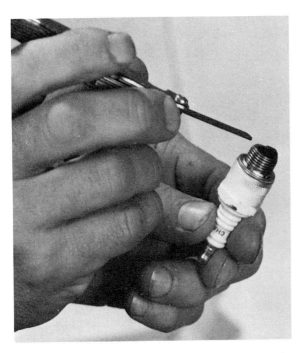

Tool for measuring "gap" between electrodes is commonly available at automotive supply stores. Stick blade of tool between electrodes. When it drags slightly, the gap is correct; owner's manual will also note correct gap.

If blade is dull, you can have your dealer sharpen it (or get a new blade). To remove the blade, use socket wrench to loosen nut, holding blade stationary with other hand. Protect hand with pad.

For better fuel consumption and for smoother running, clean the air filter. You have to remove cover to get at it.

Be sure to lubricate all points specified in owner's manual. An oil can speeds this job.

14
Safety Glazing a Storm Door

One of the more hazardous items in the average house today is the glass in a storm door, especially if you have kids. Indeed, the government recognizes this hazard and today many states have laws which mandate the use of safety-glazing materials — materials that won't break as easily as glass or, if they do, will come apart in relatively dull-edged pieces that won't cause serious injury.

Acrylic Sheeting

Of all the materials available, the easiest for the do-it-yourselfer to work with is acrylic sheeting. This is a hard, clear plastic that comes in sheets of varying thicknesses. While more expensive than glass, it is many times stronger, and once it's in you won't have to worry a lot about it breaking. One disadvantage is that it is subject to scratching much more readily than glass, but you can remove scratches with special buffing compounds manufacturers sell.

There are two major brands of acrylic sheeting commonly available: Acrylite and the better-known Plexiglas. Both are good. Check your Yellow Pages under plastics for a local outlet.

There are two ways to install acrylic sheeting in a storm door. You can install it in the metal window frame that is secured in the door or you can discard the frame and install the sheet in the storm door channels where the frame would normally rest. The latter is the easier way for the do-it-yourselfer, but neither way is really difficult.

Installation

For an in-the-frame installation, use .080 or .100 thick material. If you are going to install the material in the door channels you should use thicker material, either $^3/_{16}$ inch or $^1/_4$ inch.

It's best to remove the frame from the door to work on it and to set it on a flat surface. Frames are usually held in by clips. You just loosen the screws on the clips, turn them out of the way, and lift the frame out.

Window frame is easy to remove. Just loosen screws on clips, turn clips out of the way, and the frame slips out.

When removing window, if it is broken, wear gloves for protection.

Removing Glass

To remove the glass, use a screwdriver to pry up the ends of the spline, or gasket, that hold it in place. Then, grip the spline and pull it out, lift out glass, and discard. Clean the recesses the gasket was in. If you intend to reuse the spline, wash it in warm, soapy water. This will clean it and make it softer, easier to work with. Otherwise, get new spline of the exact diameter as the existing one. Show the old spline to a dealer.

Next, measure the frame opening. Since acrylic sheeting expands and contracts, you should cut the material slightly smaller than this opening. If the long dimension is between 12 and 36 inches, subtract $1/16$ inch from length and width; if between 37 and 48 inches, subtract $1/8$ inch.

Cutting

The sheeting may be cut in a variety of ways. You can use a circular saw equipped with a plywood cutting blade, a saber saw with a suitable blade or with a scriber you can buy for a couple of dollars. The latter is best for the do-it-yourselfer.

Measure the frame opening, taking into account the expansion and contraction of acrylic sheeting. See text for details.

To cut, place the acrylic sheeting on a flat surface with the protective-paper side up. Using a straightedge, run the scriber along the sheeting, exerting pressure. If the material is ⅛ inch or less thick, make 5 or 6 passes; make 7 to 10 passes for ³/₁₆-inch and ¼-inch thicknesses.

A most important step is sanding edges of the cut material. This prevents cracks from developing.

For do-it-yourselfers, the easiest way to cut sheeting is with a scriber you can buy. If material is less than ⅛ inch thick, make 5 or 6 passes — a few more for thicknesses over that.

After scribing, place the sheeting so the scribed line is face up and directly over a ¾-inch piece of dowel. Hold the piece on the good side with one hand, and apply pressure on the short, or waste, side, with the other. The waste should break off cleanly. If you are in a state where safety glazing is required, plan your cutting so that the safety glazing stamp is not cut away.

Next, use a small sanding block and medium grit sandpaper to remove saw marks from edges, getting them nice and smooth. Otherwise, cracks can start which will soon ruin the entire piece.

Finally, place the sheeting in the frame and reinstall the spline, forcing it in place with your fingers and a putty knife. You can also use the same tool used for splines in screens. Make sure you get the spline in tightly. Then, reinstall the frame in the door.

Before installing the sheet, it's a good idea to clean it with water and a dash of mild detergent. Use only a soft cotton flannel or jersey cloth. If tar, grease, or paint ever gets on the acrylic, use a good grade of naptha or kerosene to remove it. Periodic waxing with a good grade of automobile wax (not a cleaner-wax combination) such as Simoniz paste wax will help maintain the luster. Simply apply a thin coat and buff to a shine with a suitable cloth.

As mentioned, you can also install the new

After scribing, position scribed line over ¾-inch dowel and apply pressure on waste side. It should break off cleanly.

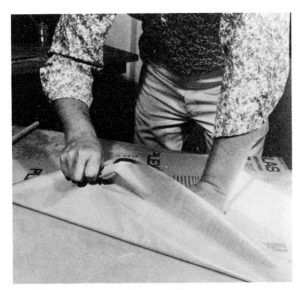

You can remove protective paper after sanding.

You can install sheeting directly in door if you wish. In this case you'd measure from recess to recess to get dimensions for cutting plastic.

Install spline in frame with fingers and putty knife. Then re-install frame in door.

Sheeting slips right into door channels. If clips don't wedge snugly against it, you can insert small strips of wood.

window in the door itself. If so, simply place it in the channels and secure it by tightening the clips. If you find that it's too loose, you can insert small wood wedges under the clips to make up the gaps, or install new spring-loaded clips.

Other Uses

If you wish, you can use acrylic sheeting for other glazing uses. For example, it works well for basement windows, providing protection against rocks and the like hurled by lawn mowers, and a degree of protection against burglars because it is hard to break or cut. You could also use it to glaze a regular multi-panel door as a security measure.

Acrylic sheeting also is good for glazing other windows, such as in garage doors. Procedure is basically the same as for glass.

15
Rebuilding with Brick

Normally, the only problem you'll have with brick will be that the mortar falls out; then you just repoint it. Other problems can occur though, usually because the brick was not installed properly in the first place. Barbecues can sag, walks heave and break, boundary walls bulge, planters collapse. If such a structure is in bad shape, the best solution is to tear down the faulty construction and rebuild. Only then can you be sure that you've solved the problem.

Many Kinds of Brick

There are many different kinds of brick in a huge array of colors and textures. If you want to try to rebuild only one section of a structure (say, one wall on a four-wall brick planter) you'll want to get new brick as close in color, texture and size to the original as possible. So loosen one brick and travel to various building supply dealers to try to get a match.

Of course, if you are leveling the structure, you can simply get what serves you best. (Before leveling, though, sketch dimensions and construction to build by.) A number of types, you'll find, predominate at building supply dealers.

Types

Standard or common brick measures 2¼ x 3¾ x 8 inches; Norman brick is 2¾ x 3¾ x 12 inches; Roman brick is 1½ x 3¾ x 12 inches. These dimensions may vary slightly in some areas; check with your local brickyard or building supply dealer early in the planning stages of your project. Brick may be solid or cored (with two rows of holes down the length of the brick).

Most brick is in the color range of the reds, buffs, and creams, varying with the type of clay used and the production process. By adding chemicals, brickmakers can produce endless variety. If you need old brick, expect to pay a premium for it; today it often costs more than new brick. But it may be possible to use the brick from the structure you've just leveled.

Bricklaying Tools

As a beginning bricklayer, your tool investment need be only minimal: a pointed trowel (10-inch will do nicely), a broad-bladed brick chisel, a hammer, a pointing tool (you can use a short length of ½-inch pipe for the job), a level, and some string. In addition, you will need a shovel for mixing mortar and a container in which to mix it; an ordinary wheelbarrow is fine, or you can do your mixing on a piece of plywood, or any other clean surface.

Foundation

The foundation for brickwork will vary depending on the project. For most projects, a concrete footing or foundation is required. The size and depth of the footing are determined partly by where you live (it must be deep enough so that it will not be disturbed by frost heaving) and partly by the size of the project. For a larger project, you may want to have the foundation put in by a contractor, then take over the job from there.

Your brick wall, or whatever, can be only as strong as the mortar that holds it together. Proper proportions for the mix are 1 part portland cement, ½ part hydrated lime, and 4 parts clean sand. You can buy mortar mix with the cement and lime already blended. Order the sand from your building supply dealer. The free kind from the beach is not suitable.

Mixing

Thoroughly blend together the dry ingredients, turning them over and over with a shovel. Scoop out a hollow in the middle of the mixture and gradually add water, mixing it in with the shovel. The working mortar should have the consistency of soft mud, and should slide easily from the trowel. Make sure it is completely mixed, with no dry spots. Also, make only as much as you can use in about a half-hour; add a little water occasionally to keep the mortar workable. If it becomes too stiff, discard it and whip up a new batch.

Brick should be damp when laid. Otherwise, it will quickly absorb the moisture from the mortar and weaken it. However, if the brick is too wet, it will dilute the mortar, causing the brick to slip. Best bet is to spray the brick lightly with a garden hose an hour or so before they are used. Just before you go to work, slightly dampen the foundation or other area where the brick is to be laid.

A Good Beginning

The pattern or bond of your brickwork depends on the project as well as your personal preference. It should be laid out with pencil and paper so that the smallest unit with which you build is a half-brick. Whether the structure is one or two bricks wide also depends on the project: a low planter box of single-brick width will be more than adequate; a high wall should be double width. Regardless of width or bond, basic bricklaying techniques are the same.

Start at Corners

If practical, start laying brick at the corners of the project first, building them up three or four courses (rows) high, dovetailed at right angles. Use the level, and square frequently to get them true. When you have built up one

When brick fails, it's usually not the brick itself that's at fault but the installation methods. Here, brick forms a retaining wall for earth.

corner, go on to the next one, lining it up with the first by means of a straightedge or line level.

With the two corners in place, push nails into the mortar between the first two courses and run a string between them. This will serve as a guide for placement of the intermediate bricks: lining them up with the string will keep the course level and the wall plumb, without bulges or curves. When the first course is laid,

move the string up and repeat the procedure for each course.

To lay the brick, scoop a slice of mortar on the trowel and place it on the foundation (or the brick course below), laying it on about ½ inch thick and long enough for two bricks (remember, you're a beginner; as your technique improves, you will be able to lay three or four bricks at a time). Furrow the mortar with the point of the trowel, making sure

To lay brick, first lay an even bed of mortar over a couple of bricks.

"Butter" the end of brick, trimming excess from eages.

Furrow the mortar with your trowel. Note guidelines. Edges of brick should be aligned with this as you build wall.

Jam buttered brick in place. Make sure there are no air pockets, and tap it in line with the end of the trowel.

the mortar is spread the full width of the brick, then "butter" the end of the brick by completely covering the end surface, and jam it firmly in place. Trim off excess mortar, butter the next brick, and set it in place against the first. Allow a ½-inch joint between bricks.

Once You're Under Way

Don't forget to keep checking with that level.

If you find your wall is running out of line, don't attempt to tap bricks back into place once they have been set. Lift up the brick, scrape off the mortar, and reset it. Otherwise, you will almost surely have a hollow spot (and thus a weakened area) in the mortar.

When you have to cut a brick to fit, first place it on a solid base. With a brick chisel and hammer, tap all around it at the cutting line, beveling the cut slightly inward. When it is

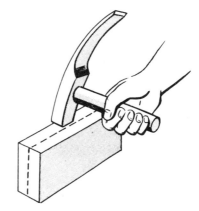

To break brick lengthwise, score all around, then rap sharply as shown.

As you build, use level to check trueness of brick on all sides. If brick is out of line, take it off and reset — don't try to tap in place.

Clean brick off with end of hammer. Process will be difficult at first, but you'll pick it up.

To cut brick, first score it deeply on all four sides with brick chisel, then hold chisel on score and rap sharply to break brick cleanly.

grooved on all sides, hold the chisel against the brick's wide face and give it a sharp blow; the brick will break apart.

As each course is completed, and before the mortar has hardened, smooth the joints with a pointer (or the ½-inch pipe mentioned earlier). Just draw the tool along the joint to produce a

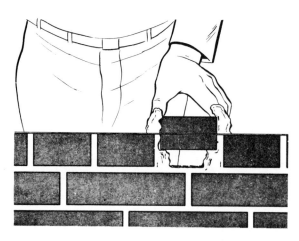

Top bricks are often set at right angles to other bricks. To set last brick, butter gap and brick on both sides, and shift into position, then trim excess.

smooth and uniform concave surface. While other types of joints (Vee's, flush, etc.) are sometimes used for decorative effects, the concave joint is by far the best for producing a water-repellent seal between bricks.

Cleaning Up

Keep a piece of damp burlap at hand, and wipe the face of the brick after each course or two to remove mortar stains. Any stains that remain after the mortar has set for several days can be removed with a solution of muriatic acid diluted with 10 parts of water. Be careful. This stuff can hurt, so wear rubber gloves and some sort of eye protection. Wet the brickwork and scrub on the solution with a stiff bristle brush. Rinse immediately with plenty of clear water. Should you splash any of the acid on your skin, wash it off immediately and thoroughly with soap and water.

For best results, treat brick gently for a couple of weeks. Mortar should set slowly, and an occasional watering, especially during hot, dry weather, will help. If your project was a barbecue pit, hold off your appetite and don't fire up for at least two or three weeks.

Once the mortar has cured, you may want to coat the brick with a colorless masonry sealer. This provides a clear weather- and water-repellent surface that will guard against crumbling mortar and water seepage. Over the years, the only further maintenance that should be required is an occasional repointing of the joints.

16
Miscellaneous Maladies

In addition to the repairs covered in other chapters, there are a number of others of a random nature that you should know about. Following is a collection of such repairs.

Wobbly Fence Post

When any kind of a post, such as a light post, is set in a hole in the ground it is susceptible to becoming loose and wobbly. The answer is to take the post and seat it in concrete.

After taking the post out, use a manual post-hole digger, which can be rented, to widen the diameter of the posthole. Dig it 3 to 4 inches deeper than it was. Fill this extra 3 or 4 inches with gravel for drainage. Then set the post in place. Fill the hole with a premixed concrete. You can keep the post true — straight — as you pour by using boards, if dealing with wood, staked into the ground; or, if using metal posts, prop the post in position with heavy blocks. The concrete at the top should be beveled, or sloped, with a trowel to allow water to run off. (See illustrations page 86.)

If you need a new post for any reason, get one that has been soaked in preservative.

Rotting Wood

Various fungi can cause wood to decay and weaken. A few years ago, the solution was to replace the offending part, or cut it out and replace with new wood. Today, you needn't do that. Just obtain a container of Git Rot. To use, drill a few holes in the rotted sections and inject this material into them. It will seep into the wood and turn to a hard substance that, in effect, turns the wood to plastic and prevents further damage. Boatmen swear by it. You can buy it at lumberyards and marine supply stores.

Balky Doors

Exterior doors that don't open or close easily usually suffer from the same

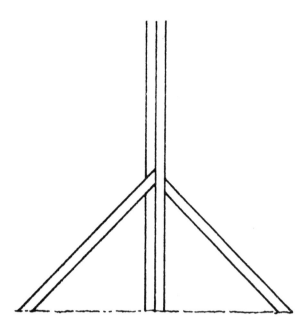

Nailing boards to wood post will hold it true while pouring concrete around it. Blocks can be used to brace metal post.

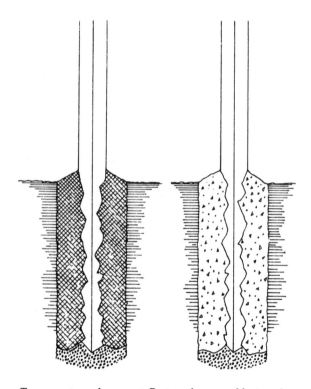

Two ways to anchor a post. Post can be secured by tamping soil down around it. Soil is sloped at top for water runoff. Concrete is used to secure post (right). Bottoms of both holes are lined with gravel for drainage.

malady as interior ones: The hinges are loose. Simply tighten the hinge screws and the problem should be solved.

Stains

Patios, driveways and, walks are susceptible to a wide variety of stains. The main idea in removing any kind of stain is to get at it fast. The longer it has to set, the harder the time you'll have removing it.

If grease and fats are the problem, scrub them with boiling hot water and dishwasher detergent; also work on the stain with a paint scraper or putty knife. Then, pour undiluted detergent on the stains and let stand for 15 minutes. Scrub again vigorously with a brush as you pour measured amounts of boiling rinse water on. Repeat the procedure if necessary.

Dried Paint: Dried paint is tougher. One fairly successful way to attack it is with a paint and varnish remover. The jellied type is applied with a putty knife, allowed to stand, then washed away. Another treatment is usually called for, and it does leave the concrete slightly lighter than surrounding areas. To avoid this you can use a slower but just as good method, using one of the powdered garage floor cleaners available at auto supply stores. With these cleaners, the stained area is wetted down, the powder sprinkled on, let stand for 15 minutes, then hosed off. You can also use this powder for removing oil stains. Before using any of these products, however, be sure to read the label. Some, for example, will ruin asphalt.

Cleaning Stucco

Stucco may be brightened and discolorations may be concealed by painting with cement-water paint. Since the cement-water paint will fill hairline cracks, only serious defects need be pointed up. The surface should be cleaned according to manufacturer's directions before applying a paint. In hot, dry weather, the surface should be dampened before application. If the stucco has been painted with an oil-base paint, the cement-water paint will not adhere well, and an oil-base paint or a resin-emulsion paint should be used for repainting.

If cracks are big, they should be repaired right away. If they are not noticeable and seem to be doing no damage, repairs may be postponed, since the patches do stand out like a sore thumb.

Before patching, clean out the cracks with a wire brush or whisk broom thoroughly and chip them out to the shape of an inverted V (larger at bottom of crack then top) in order to key the patches securely to the old work. Be sure to remove all dust and loose particles.

In patching new cracks in the stucco, it is desirable to use the same brand of cement and the same mix proportions as the original work. If the previous mixture cannot be determined, it is usually safe to use a 1 to 3 mixture, containing 1 part cement, 3 parts sand, and $\frac{1}{10}$ part finely divided materials, such as hydrated lime, measured by volume.

The mortar should contain just enough water to make a fairly dry mixture about the consistency of putty. Before applying, wet the surface

Stains on masonry can be removed with a variety of strong preparations, but the important rule is to get at the removal procedure as quickly as possible.

Cracks in Stucco

Cracks are among the most common defects found in stucco. They may be merely hairline cracks or large enough to let water in. This may damage the underlying structure and interior walls.

Hairline cracks usually develop if a stucco mixture is wrong or if the mix material is inferior. They can also be caused by too rapid drying of freshly applied stucco. Large cracks are usually caused by settling of house walls or movement within the walls caused by incorrectly constructed foundation walls or poorly designed framing in the superstructure of the house.

Also, stucco over brick, stone, or similar materials is liable to crack, especially around chimneys, because it has a different rate of expansion and contraction than the material that it covers, and a shearing or "crawling" effect takes place.

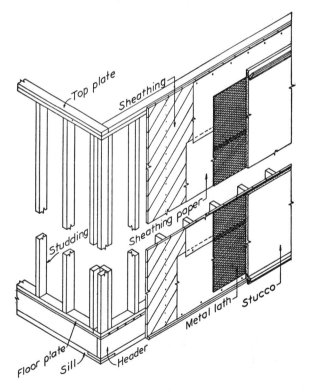

How a stucco wall is constructed. Metal lath (mesh) is secured to house sheathing, then stucco (a cement mixture) is troweled onto mesh. It is possible to put on a complete new coat of stucco, but it's a difficult job for a non-professional.

thoroughly. Apply mortar like a caulking material; that is, rammed and tamped in well so as to make complete contact and form a secure bond. Since cracks will likely show up badly after pointing work is finished, it may be necessary to paint the entire surface with a cement-water or latex paint. Keep the new work wet for several days after it has hardened to increase mortar strength. It is also advisable to hang a tarpaulin or similar covering over the completed work to protect it from direct exposure to the sun and drying winds.

Cure for a Beat-up Basement Entry

If the basement door on your home has seen better days and has been a constant lure for your handyman skills, it may be time to replace it. Today, the job is relatively simple. A number of manufacturers make steel doors that you assemble like an erector set, then install on the old sidewalls.

Preliminary Steps

First step is to remove the old door. Here, a crowbar and hammer are useful. When the door is off, examine the walls. If they slope, it is advisable to pound them down level with a sledgehammer and recap them with new masonry.

Door can be removed with crowbar. When it is off, examine sidewalls for their condition and position.

Set the frame of the door in place in final position, blocking it up with bricks or wood as necessary. Mark where the top meets the wall.

BEFORE: Basement entry has seen better days.

AFTER: New metal door will last for years. It can be painted to suit house color.

If you have wood siding, it is cut out so that the flange on the frame can slip in under it for watertightness.

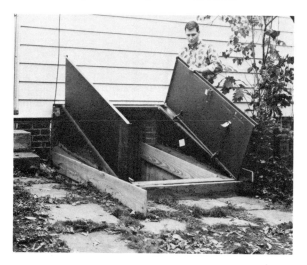

The door hooks onto the frame easily. Torsion bars enable you to open it easily.

After assembling the framework of the new door, slide it onto the sidewalls, and mark the siding where the top falls. Then, using a saw, cut the siding so the header flange on the unit will fit up between the sheathing and the siding. If your home is brick or masonry, the frame rests against the material and is caulked and flashed (made watertight).

Next, build a simple board form around the old sidewalls and set the frame back in place. Block the frame up to the correct height with

Simple board forms around walls enable you to cement door in place easily. Check doors for proper alignment before the concrete sets.

bricks. Mix concrete and use a trowel to fill in around and under the frame. Also embed the screws with the spring nuts that are supplied. These lock the frame to the capping.

Doors

Attach the doors to the frame. Check to see that the bottom edges of both doors form a straight line. If not, move the front of the unit left or right for proper alignment.

When the concrete has set, engage the tor-

If you wish, you can create a basement entry. This entails going through foundation wall.

sion bars in clips or the side pieces as detailed in manufacturer's instructions. (Torsion bars make the door easy to open and close.)

Remove the form boards. Apply caulk around the outside of the door where it joins the masonry and house wall. The final step is to paint the entry to suit using an enamel for metal.

Incidentally, if you don't have a basement door now, but would like one, you can build a stairwell, punch a hole in the foundation for a basement-wall door, and install the entry as described.

Rusty Tools

Rust is the enemy of all metal, including tools. Let go long enough, it will eat through the metal and make the tool useless.

The best answer we've found is one of the rust-removing products made especially for the purpose, such as Naval Jelly. This has the consistency of molasses. All you do is pour the product on the rusty parts, spreading it on with a brush or rag, and wait. If the rust is minimal, wait 10 minutes. Then rinse the substance away with clear water and all the rust will be gone. If the rust is particularly heavy, just leave the product on for a longer period of time — say 2 or 3 hours, then rinse. And that's all there is to it.

Efflorescence

Efflorescence is the name given to the condition where natural salt in masonry — stucco, brick, mortar — is deposited on the surface. It usually is white, but may be the color of the particular form of masonry it's on.

Efflorescence comes about because excessive water in the masonry dissolves the salts. The water migrates to the surface, evaporates, and the salt is left. Usually, efflorescence is found on new masonry, where a good deal of water is present; as the work gets older the accumulation disappears.

Removal: The first way to remove efflorescence is simply to brush it vigorously with a stiff fiber or wire brush. If this doesn't do it, make a mixture of muriatic acid and water. The solution should be one part muriatic acid to 6-10 parts water. Just dip the brush in the solution and scrub vigorously, avoiding the mortar joints as much as possible. When finished, rinse the area with clear water. Then wash again with an ammonia and water solution (one part ammonia to two gallons of water) to remove every trace of the acid. Efflorescence may appear again from time to time but will eventually disappear as all the salts in the masonry are depleted.

One caution: Handle muriatic acid with care. It's possible to be burned by it, so wear gloves and glasses.

Killing Termites

One of the least loved insects in the world is the termite. And it is probably one of the most feared. In many people's minds, the name termite almost immediately conjures up an image of a house coming down around one's ears.

While we've yet to hear of this happening, termites can cause considerable damage, and should be counterattacked promptly. Most experts feel that it is not a job for a handyman. The cure involves pumping chemicals (after drilling many holes) around the house foundation, and it is both tiresome and potentially hazardous because of the chemicals used. Indeed, one of them used for years, chlordane, was recently banned from use in a number of areas of the United States.

Recognizing Termites

While handling termites may not be the problem for the handyman, he or she can play an important role just by spotting them so professionals can treat the house.

Termites are often confused with flying ants, but the anatomies differ sharply. Ants have wasp waists and different-size wings. Termites have no waist lines, and wings are all the same size.

Termites commonly enter a house by means of mud tubes that they build between the soil where they live and the house framing. These tubes are usually flattish, from ¼ to ½ inch wide. Look for them on foundation walls, in cracks in the foundation, on pipes, on posts — on anything that leads to wood.

Not seeing tubes is no guarantee that termites aren't present. Sometimes the tubes are hidden. We know of one case where the tubes were behind a thin coat of mortar that had been improperly applied to a block foundation wall. They were effectively out of sight.

Check with Awl

One way of identifying their presence is to spot them flying around. Another way is to poke the various wood parts of your home — especially wood close to the foundation wall and ground — with an awl or icepick. If termites are present, and have had time to dine for awhile, the tool will penetrate easily. What has happened is that the termites have characteristically eaten a network of tunnel-like tubes in the wood, greatly weakening it.

Similar to termite damage, but clearly distinguishable, is that caused by "dry rot." Actually a misnomer, dry rot is a condition of wood caused by fungi in damp wood. Evidence of dry rot is that the wood is crumbly — there are no tunnels separated by layers of sound wood. Handling dry rot was covered earlier (see page 85).

Combatting the Pests

To survive, termites need moisture so after feasting on house framing they'll make their way back through the tunnels to the earth, where the moisture is. The way to kill them is to create an insecticide barrier between that wood and the earth with its life-giving moisture. It's also the way to prevent them from traveling back through the tubes. It's a wall they can't penetrate.

To do this properly, it is necessary to saturate the ground on both sides of the foundation with chemicals. To do this, the professional exterminator first drills a shallow trench next to the foundation wall, then bores deep holes about 18 inches apart into the earth in the

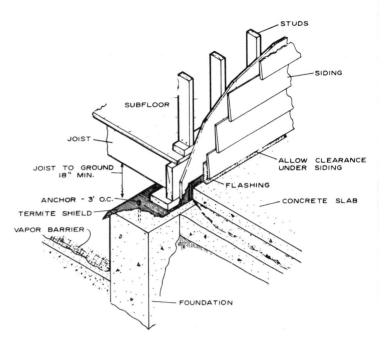

Best way to protect house against termites is by installing termite shield over foundation during construction. (The termite shield is the dark portion in picture.)

trench. Then, into these holes he pressure-pumps insecticide. Wherever there is concrete interfering with this trench digging (such as a walk), the pro drills holes with an enormous (1½-foot) carbide drill through the concrete, then deep into the earth. Then he pumps the insecticide in.

Essentially the same routine must be followed inside the house. Holes are drilled in the floor about 18 inches apart, and insecticide is pumped in. The job can be done without major damage to the house or grounds. Outside, holes in concrete are filled with mortar plugs. Inside the pro has tricks (such as a cutter that can remove perfect plug-size pieces of flooring for replacement) to leave it undamaged.

Get the Right Pro

If you need to hire a professional for the job, get at least three bids and check out the man you wish to hire at your local Better Business Bureau. It's a sad fact that the industry is swarming with rip-off artists.

Broken Handles

Handles on hoes, rakes, shovels and the like often break. Replacement rather than repair of the existing handle is the solution. Check first, though, to see if you have a guarantee on the tool — you may be able to get a new handle free. Nurseries, hardware stores, and garden supply outfits usually carry a supply of handles from which you can select the right one.

Such tools usually have a simple anatomy: The handle is tapered at the bottom and fits snugly into a metal tube-like affair or ferrule. It is held securely there by one or more rivets.

The broken piece in the ferrule must be taken out. To get the rivet(s) off, use a hacksaw to saw off the head, then knock the shank part out with a punch (a piece of metal shaped like a nail) and hammer. It's likely that the head will be locked in securely. To remove it, lock the protruding portion of the handle in a vise and tap the head off with a hammer.

Fit New Handle in Ferrule: Insert the new handle into the ferrule, using sandpaper and rasp if necessary to make it fit. Then, using the holes in the ferrule as a guide, mark the handle where the holes fall. Remove the handle, clamp it in a vise and drill holes for new rivets. Reinsert the handle, slip rivets in place. (Rivets are available in various sizes at hardware stores.) Place the tool on a flat, solid surface and use the ball end of a ball peen hammer to mushroom the headless end of each rivet so it locks the handle securely in place. Another way to

Handles of tools are commonly held on by rivets in ferrule. To remove handle, punch rivets out.

First step in disassembling a faucet is to loosen cap nut. A wrench works best, but you can use pliers.

secure the handle is with short bolts and nuts; when nuts are in place, mushroom the nut with a hammer, creating a rivet in the process.

Leaky Faucet

Handymen have a way of letting outside faucets drip forever, whereas they wouldn't tolerate the same condition in an inside faucet. Perhaps it's because they think it involves some mysterious repair work. Actually, repairing faucets inside or outside the house is about the same, and just as easy.

First step is to turn off the water. If you know which valve controls the outside faucet, fine — just turn it off. If you are not sure, you can turn on the water and try various valves until one does the trick. If you can't locate the valve (and sometimes they are difficult to find), turn off the main valve, which will be by your water meter. This will shut off everything in the house, but if you have all your repair materials and tools at hand you'll have the water flowing again within 10 minutes.

On some faucets, you also have to loosen stem nut, as shown. Then just turn the faucet in the "On" position, round and round, until the assembly comes out.

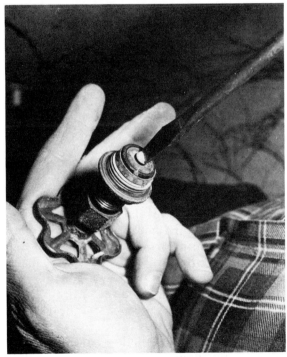

Washer is held on by a little screw. Loosen with screwdriver. If screw balks, use a couple of drops of penetrating oil and wait five minutes before trying.

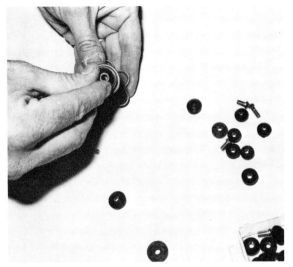

Match new washer with old, and screw in place. The faucet's repaired.

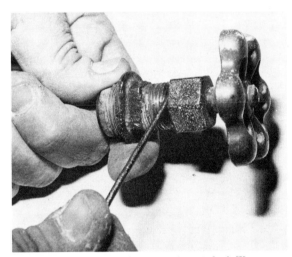

Leak around cap nut indicates packing is bad. Wrap new packing under nut, and clip off excess.

The problem is likely caused by a worn or chewed up washer. To get at it, disassemble the faucet. Use a wrench to turn the big nut (cap nut) that the handle stem disappears into. With this loose, turn the faucet to the ON position until it screws out of the faucet body mounted in the wall. On the bottom of this assembly will be the culprit, the washer — held on by a little screw.

Remove the screw holding the washer on, then simply replace it with one the same size. Then reinstall the faucet. The washer should solve the problem. If it doesn't, it may be that the faucet seat — the metal hole the washer sits in and seals — needs to be reamed, made smooth so the washer can seal against it well. You can pick up a seat-reaming kit for a dollar or so. Simple instructions are on the package.

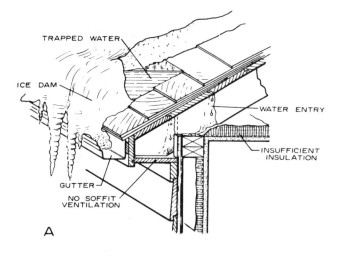

A

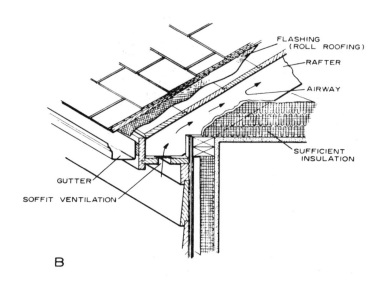

B

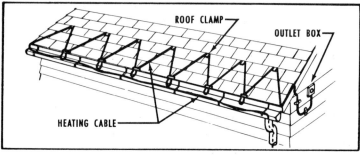

On some faucets, disassembly involves taking off the handle, then loosening the stem sticking into the wall by turning it with a wrench. This type is shown in the photos.

Leak around Cap Nut: Sometimes, you'll find water leaking out around the top of the cap nut. This means that the packing is worn. Packing is graphite-impregnated string that is wrapped around the faucet stem where the cap nut goes to provide a watertight seal.

The answer is to replace it. The best packing today is plastic. It is soft and malleable, better than string. Simply wrap it three or four times under the cap nut and cut the rest off. Tighten the cap nut and turn on the water. Still leak? Try some more packing.

You may find it difficult to disassemble your faucet. Years of rust and corrosion can really make parts hard to turn. If this is a problem, first squirt penetrating oil, available in small cans at hardware stores, wherever metal meets metal on the parts you want to turn. Give the oil 5 or 10 minutes to work, then turn. You should be able to — easily.

Ice Dams

When the overhanging portion of the roof is cold (the part above the soffit in Fig. A) and the rest of the roof is warm, ice dams can result. After a snowfall, the water is melted by the warm part of the roof, but runs down to the overhanging part and freezes. This creates an ice dam. Subsequent water melts, builds up, then backs up under shingle or fascia and gets inside house, where damage can be extensive.

There are a couple of causes: usually insufficient ventilation through the soffit, and inadequate or no insulation under the roof. Warm air from the house will keep the water melting indefinitely.

To solve the problem, you can install adequate insulation (6 inches) and provide ventilation in the soffit so the entire roof will be cold. It also helps if you install flashing under shingles, but if this isn't practical you can manage without it. Another solution is even simpler: install electric cable along the edge of the roof. This will keep the edge of the roof warm so that ice can't form.

Index